BECOMING

you

A Guide To Designing A Life You Love

rebecca cafiero

Published by Elevate Publications

Cover photo by Molly McCauley

ISBN: 9798629946120

For my husband, Igino, whose love and belief in me
makes all things possible.

For my children, Luca and Valentina,
who show me daily how to simply BE.

"Do whatever you need to do to BE happy,
because when you are happy, you can do anything".

Contents

CHAPTER 1

Becoming Me

*"You can't really know where you are going
until you know where you have been."*

– MAYA ANGELOU

To really understand my journey to become the woman in progress I am today, let's go back to where it all started. You can get so much value out of this book without my story, but if you really want to understand the successes, the failures, the growth, and the tears that led to me becoming me, read on.

I was born in a tiny rural Oregon town of about 3,000. The major industry is still timber and fishing. It's a blue-collar existence that often feels so far removed from the life I live now. My dad is a fisherman, and my stepdad's a water well driller. I'm the oldest of three with two younger brothers.

I'm part of a huge extended family, most that lived within a 30-minute drive. I grew up with more than 40 aunts and uncles and more than 70 first cousins. There was a lot of love and an equal amount of craziness and family drama.

My tiny world imploded at five when my dad left. As a fisherman, he was gone for weeks at a time already, but divorce meant an entirely different type of absence.

I don't remember the word divorce being used, but oh, I remember that day. It's one of my earliest memories – sitting in my bedroom reading my books when my mom came to tell me we wouldn't be living as a family anymore. She said all of the loving things about it not being my fault, but I was too busy listening to the sound of my heart cracking from the inside to let her words sink in.

I didn't know if I'd ever see my dad again. My larger-than-life, charismatic daddy, who had blue twinkling eyes, a scratchy mustache, and legendary skills to tell a tall tale.

That night, I stayed awake listening to the sounds of my mom going to bed. I crept out of bed, moving through the shadows to each picture frame. With my little thumbs, I carefully removed the photos of my dad from the frames and slid them silently into an envelope I hid in a book. It was my self-preservation to ensure I wouldn't forget what he looked like.

Though I couldn't have defined it then, that day was when the idea of independence began to take root in me. I realized at that pivotal time that people don't always stay. It's a lesson, a story, that's played an ongoing role in my life.

The ripple effect from that day didn't stop. We moved out of the house I was born in to a small duplex close to my grandparents. My mom went back to school after having left college to get married at 18. She started a part-time job. My young grasp on life slipped before I understood what stability even meant.

But life went on. Just a different life than the one I had imagined. Kindergarten started, and so did my fear of doing something wrong. I thought, "If I'm a good enough girl, if I behave, if I do all the right things, then maybe people won't leave."

Even though my mom was emphatic about telling me that my dad leaving wasn't my fault, that it had nothing to do with me, a part of me still felt like I could have done something differently. I could have been better. And that need to please, to be good, to deserve the love of the people around me, took hold. It was my way of making sense of something that made no sense.

And my childhood was wonderful yet tough. I was a happy child who was sometimes prone to anxiety and nightmares, usually the result of over-hearing adult conversations like, "This is a bad month. I don't know how we're going to pay the bills," or "I just can't deal with her."

I knew we were poor, though my mom's wonderful home cooking, insist-ence on manners, and ability to sew shielded me from much of the trauma I could have experienced from those early years when we qualified for public assistance, or welfare. But not always.

I remember a day, as a kindergartner, that a cruel third grader taunted me about my hand-me-down clothes, telling me I was ugly. Her words hurt, but she hit a nerve when she started insulting my mom. The tears flew.

To this day, while I pride myself on talking through conflict and not letting much get to me, witnessing anything that resembles bullying is sure to boil my blood. Even now, I want to go back and protect that little girl who cried her way off the bus, to wipe her tears, to tell her she's beautiful and loved and enough. And then, tell the older girl who bullied me that she is beautiful, smart, kind, and important.

While I missed my dad terribly between his visits, my mom was my rock. I worshipped her, defended her, and thought she was the best human alive. Even as a tween, I proudly announced that she was my best friend.

My mom got remarried and we moved a town over to my stepdad's farm. Growing up with chores like feeding the cows, yard work, and garden work and having acres to roam is something I'll always cherish. It taught me that I had value, how it felt to contribute, and that I was capable.

We had salsa-making parties, picked fruit to freeze for winter, and canned tomatoes and tuna. I often rode my bike miles to school or the nearby market to buy candy. Our life was closer to Little House on the Prairie than it is to my life now, living in Silicon Valley.

Life became more stable, and while I was still a pleaser, I also fought constantly with my younger brother. At the time, he just annoyed me in the unique way that a younger brother can do – with an irritating look, touching any of my coveted treasures, or being in the bathroom when I wanted to curl my bangs (this was the late 1980s, and bangs were high and stiff with AquaNet).

We got spanked or grounded occasionally, usually for fighting with each other. Or for me, *never* being able to resist getting the last word. My mouth got me in trouble more than once, not for curse words, but for constantly asking questions and for always talking – in class, at home, or on the bus. I usually had an opinion, and if I didn't, I had questions!

I was involved in everything at school, every extracurricular activity, winning every award, feeling like my self-worth came from all of the things I was doing and the awards or accolades I was receiving. It was absolutely an obsession, and it was not to be competitive with other people, it was really to be competitive with myself, feeling as though I needed these things to feel deserving, to feel worthy.

That quest for self-worth grew when I turned 12 and started working. I have always loved making money for the feeling of independence it created to make my own spending decisions, as well as the validation I got from my happy babysitting, landscaping, or car-washing clients. There was a security to making money, to having options. It meant freedom, even if only a small taste.

I didn't realize I was an accidental entrepreneur, offering to add on car washing to my babysitting clients or combining data entry with babysitting. In fact, I had no desire to own my own business after watching my parents, both small business owners.

I watched their businesses being run by outside forces, whether tax deadlines, the weather, or the fishing season. They didn't feel like they had control over the time they were working or the money (or lack thereof) that a bad season would result in. I'd hear the conversations my parents would have, and from my angle, it seemed like everything was out of control. I remember thinking, "I am so willing to work hard, but I don't want to own my own business because your business runs you."

As I entered young adulthood, my passions really bloomed. Poring over electives and extracurricular clubs in high school was something I *savored!* I was in yearbook and newspaper, theater and volunteer clubs, leadership and sports. It was at that time that I started to realize I loved writing, journalism, speaking, and having a voice so I could create an impact. As an adult, I realize I'm passionate about passion.

During high school, I fell in love with customer service when I landed my first waitressing job. I loved that the better I served the customer, the more money I could make. It validated me as a hard worker while providing the financial independence I so craved.

But the most valuable thing I learned in high school was resourcefulness. It's still the most valuable skill I learned at a young age. It was born from my desire to do everything. I wanted to go to every summer camp, from cheerleading to yearbook to leadership because I craved learning, experience, and independence. I wanted to see the world.

Those camps were my first foray into travel, to seeing a world different than the one in which I grew up. I spent most of my first 18 years in the small town my parents had been born in and that my grandparents and cousins lived in. People didn't seem to leave. Most of my cousins and my family and the people I knew had never lived outside of our small, rural county, and I had this desire to go out and see the world.

Sometimes I found my way out by reading, constantly escaping in books. I snuck them in bed and into the bathroom. I got a bloody nose in elementary school from walking into a tetherball pole with my nose buried in a book! Books are still something I love, though I find myself spending more time reading to learn rather than reading to escape.

When I was applying to these camps as a 14 or 15-year-old, my parents often said, "Well, we can't afford that," or "That's not an option." I realized that money was the limiting factor early on, so I decided to figure out a way to make this happen. The solution? Apply for scholarships. This was before the Internet, so I found books of scholarships in my high school guidance office, and I started to apply for things via the mail. I found non-profit groups that offered youth scholarships and I applied for them.

I learned at that early age that it's not about your resources, it's about your resourcefulness. If I wanted to do things, I had to be creative. Not having money was not going to stop me because I could figure out a way to make it work, whether it was washing cars or candy sale drives to pay for cheerleading camp or entering a speech content to win a scholarship for a camp that I wanted to attend.

My senior year, I had a falling out with my parents over a guy. Right after my 18th birthday, I ended up living on my own and being entirely financially independent.

That was a huge, scary responsibility at 18. It was terrifying to be so untethered and feel unsupported, but it was also an incredible learning lesson to figure out life and finances and to put those skills of hard work and resourcefulness I learned into action. I had to pay the bills.

My first big hurdle was trying to figure out how to get college paid for! I had applied to schools, mostly private schools, that I was able to afford with my parents' help. When I no longer had that financial support, life was really turned upside down.

I started applying to state schools that I could personally afford. I applied to West Point Military Academy, where I set a record in their physical aptitude exam for the flexed arm hang. Though I was small, I've always believed in my strength and I loved a challenge. If you said, "You can't do this," I would show you. At that age, it was about proving to myself that I could do it, whatever it was.

I decided that after not being able to live within what I considered to be "parental control," West Point was probably not the best option. Instead, I went to one of the most liberal schools in the United States, the University of Oregon.

I loved the fact that I was only an hour away from my parents, which was a good distance. It strengthened our relationship again. College definitely included some bumpy years, but I could go home on the weekends.

I continued to work my way through school by waitressing on weekends and balancing my school week between classes, homework, and work study. I worked as a graphic designer for the school before landing a job at the university's daily newspaper, where I learned more about writing and deadlines than in any classroom.

I graduated in 2002 and moved the next *day* to Los Angeles, all of my belongings crammed into my Honda Civic, all of my furniture towed in a small trailer. I was ready to start the next chapter of my life.

My plan, coming out of graduation, was not to pursue journalism, because a career as a reporter paid the same as minimum wage. And though I loved the fast paced, deadline-centric culture of the newsroom, having to have additional jobs to pay my rent got a bit old after three years of it in college.

Instead, I decided to go to law school. I had always loved debate, formulating my arguments, and the safety of logic. So I moved to L.A. with the intention of establishing residency to go to UCLA or one of the California state schools.

That year I joined thousands of other twenty somethings moving to L.A. from small towns. I did odd makeup jobs, modeling and commercial jobs, worked during the day in a real estate office, worked nights doing liquor promotions, then bartended on the weekends.

At any given time I was doing nine things, but it allowed me to pay off what little student debt I had taken out less than six months after graduation. Debt was an obligation, and I didn't want to owe anyone anything.

After all that, I ended up going into real estate, something I'd never planned on doing. I had no desire to do sales. But the ability to ask questions I'd learned through journalism combined with my passion for people, learning, and solving problems equated to some very natural sales ability!

My boyfriend at the time had an interview for a new home real estate development company in Las Vegas. By a strange twist of luck, I ended up getting an interview as well – the next day! That night I bought myself a $60 suit on clearance to wear to the interview, and I got the job!

I drove back from Las Vegas to L.A. that day, subleased my apartment, sold half of my things on Craigslist, rented a U-Haul, packed it up, and found an apartment online. I filled out all the paperwork and was back in Vegas in less than 48 hours. When I decide to do something, I am all in.

At 23, I moved to Las Vegas with my boyfriend, both of us with promising jobs making six figures a year. This was in 2003 at the height of the real estate market. It was nuts, and Las Vegas was the epicenter of the real estate boom.

Right before I started my company training in sales, I'd heard about another recent college graduate who was making a couple hundred thousand dollars a year her first year selling. I asked my future boss, "Is it really possible to make $100,000 year at 24 years old?" And he said, "Well, not only is it possible, but if you only make $100,000 a year, that means you're not hitting your quotas and you'll actually be fired." That blew my mind. My money mindset was so different back then, and I thought you could only make that kind of money if you were a doctor or lawyer.

So I worked like a dog. I didn't know what I didn't know, so I assumed that every person walking through our sales office door would buy a house from me. Most of them did. My first 10 weeks, I sold more than $22 million in real estate, about 40% of the sales volume in an office of 10 salespeople.

At one point my boss ordered me to take a day off, because I'd worked without a break for months. But I'd gone from working four jobs to earn $40,000 a year to making over $200,000 the next. I had a taste of what earning real income was like and wanted more.

I bought my first house, bought an investment condo, and maxed out my 401k. I took a lot of pride in all of this because it felt like security to me. I figured I was just going to work, work, work, because I don't know how long it was going to last.

At 26, I reached the point where I was making incredible money, living in my dream home and had a great job where my skills were validated. I won awards. But the harder I worked and the more I earned, the bigger the hole in my life grew. And I didn't know how to fill it.

So I hired my first life coach. And that first session was nothing like I expected. She asked me about my future and my plans, and I proudly recited off an oral version of my resume, what my next ten years looked like, and my path to manager and vice president and so on – my path of success. It sounded very impressive. At least I thought it did. And at the end of it, she said, "Okay, but what do you actually want?"

I broke down sobbing. I realized I didn't really want any of this. I was doing it for security, but it wasn't what my heart was begging for. I wanted joy, passion, excitement, travel, purpose, and growth.

Over the next few months working with her, I tapped into joy. I started to work a little bit less, taking one day off a week, cutting my 14-hour days to 10.

I began to do the things that were calling to my soul. I enrolled in an evening photography class and a theater class. And I started circus school lessons to learn the aerial silks. I also began to travel. I was doing all these things to infuse joy into my life, and it definitely helped.

But the more joy I infused, the more I felt like I was adding on joy condiments with a main course made out of cardboard. It helped, but it didn't materially change how I felt.

Then 2007 happened and the real estate market began to decline. I have always been a person who believes you make your own destiny and your own fortune. You can figure out a way. So I was working hard to ignore the people saying, "The market's falling apart."

I was still making really good money, though I knew what I was doing wasn't fulfilling me. But the added joy had given me clarity that it wasn't just my career, but my five-year relationship that felt like the cardboard main course. I realized that if I wanted to have a long, happy, and passionate life, that relationship was not going to be able to be a part of it. And we'd been married for just over a year.

It wasn't a horrible relationship. It was just that he and I were not compatible for long-term joy. I began recoiling at the idea of having children, something I'd always wanted. And when I dug deep into that mindset change, I realized I just didn't want to have children with him. It was a *hard* realization, to consider myself someone who always succeeded with hard work and positive mindset and to feel I had failed myself, and him, in choosing a partner.

I vowed to myself to never fail at marriage. And I had picked a partner who would never leave me, who could never break me, in the way I'd seen my dad leave, in the way I'd felt broken. And many nights, I wept to myself, at the pain I was going through, at the pain I caused him, and also, at the realization that I could still pursue the light of joy on the other side of the dark tunnel of divorce.

So I ended that relationship with a lot of pain. At that time, I wrote out a list of qualities that I wanted in a partner: someone who was curious about knowledge, someone who always wanted to improve themselves, someone who is humble, someone who is trustworthy, someone who loves to explore the world, to travel, someone who is giving, someone who is open, patient, and sweet.

I thought, before I get into my next relationship, I'm going to make sure the next person has these non-negotiable qualities.

In 2008, after ending this relationship, I could no longer ignore the crashing real estate and financial markets. As my sales income was cut in half and dwindling slowly each month, I realized, "I have nothing to show for the last five years of hard work but experience." Most of the assets that I had accumulated, the rental properties, the land, and my stocks, were losing value as fast as my income.

In addition to experience, those dog years in real estate gave me some of my best lifelong friends. My real estate mentee turned friend turned roommate said to me, "Rebecca, you're such a hard worker. You should be working for yourself."

She had grown up with a father who was an architect and entrepreneur and asked me why I wasn't working for myself. And I replied, "No, I don't want that risk."

I was ready to take on the risk of leaving Las Vegas and changing employers to a smaller real estate developer in California that had been recruiting me for most of the year. They told me I should base myself out of Palm Springs, a central location to the large territory from Orange County to Phoenix I'd be covering, and I began to redesign my life.

I'd never been to Palm Springs, but I found a brand new modern house online, researched gyms and grocery stores, and calendared out events I'd love to attend in my soon-to-be new city.

The real estate market was still in decline and the company that had hired me as their Vice President of Sales and Marketing was not straightforward with me about their balance sheets. But I was looking for a change, and in my excitement to start over in every way, I didn't ask all the questions I should have.

Six months after I left the secure job in Las Vegas and took this new job in California, the company closed their doors. I learned a valuable lesson: that you can't look to a corporation to take care of you. At the end of the day, as much as we can give our best years and efforts to a company, they're going to do what's best for them first.

I went through a few more real estate jobs, just working to tread water as my savings disappeared. One month, to pay the bills, I sold the furniture I had in storage. The next month, I pawned the silver coins my parents and grandparents had given me when I was a child.

Between a toxic work situation and an even more toxic rebound relation-ship after my divorce that drained me emotionally and financially, I didn't think life could get worse. I had to borrow money from my parents to take out a restraining order after the ex-boyfriend had threatened me, often calling me hundreds of times in the middle of the night until I'd finally turn off my phone.

One night, in complete despair, I cried so hard that I audio recorded my sobs, knowing anytime I felt like life was difficult, I would know I had survived this moment and that I could go on. I knew that this was rock bottom.

But it wasn't.

A few months later, I met and began dating a wonderful young man, Amir. He was intelligent, handsome, and fun, and our first short coffee date turned into a long walk on the beach, playing games at an arcade, and then a spontaneous dinner. We grew a friendship and then a romance over day dates like hot yoga, soccer, and beach walks for weeks before we went on an evening date. He was easy to be around and there were no expectations or pressure except to enjoy ourselves during our time together.

I felt like I was getting a handle back on life. More importantly, my natural state of positivity and possibility was re-emerging. The anxiety I held and the gray clouds over my future were beginning to dissipate.

And then Amir began to have stomach pains. He had blood work done and nothing seemed amiss. Always loving research and health, I made recommendations for him to cut out coffee in case it was acid reflux. After a week of no improvement, he started throwing up after Mother's Day lunch and didn't stop for two days.

It was Stage IV intestinal cancer.

You don't imagine the first time you meet your boyfriend's mom, it'll be the day he's starting chemotherapy, that your first one-on-one conversation with her will be telling you that it's OK to leave... because this is about to get *hard*. Because it's not what you signed up for.

But I didn't leave. Because he hadn't chosen this. And after a few hard years, before meeting him, I realized I'd begun to doubt myself, my positivity, my resourcefulness, my magic. And he had rekindled my belief.

I knew I was going to stay for two reasons. First, because I had a belief that I could pour all of my positivity, my research, my energy, and my love into him and it just *might* save him. It might defy all odds. It might be enough to prove wrong a diagnosis of one to three years left to live – a diagnosis that gave no chance of survival.

And the second reason? Because I needed to prove to myself that I was good. After divorce, toxic jobs, and toxic relationships, I had lost the belief in myself, in the idea that life was happening for me. Because for the past few years, it seemed like it was happening *to* me. Amir had sparked my belief again and I knew that giving him my magic and belief in him could fan that spark into a flame.

The next year was one of the hardest things I've ever gone through. It was also one of the most beautiful gifts, because it showed me the value of life. It showed me the priority of what is *really* important – connection, laughter, family, time, and choice.

So much of the time I spent just *being* – sitting with him when he was in chemo or staying overnight at the hospital – and it was time I look back on with so much happiness. I would read to him or we would play chess, just being in the moment, talking and laughing. I found a television in the hospital and brought in a PlayStation so we could play video games. We received "noise violations" and scoldings from the nurses because we'd be laughing so hard that we'd disturb the patients in adjoining rooms. We were celebrating every moment.

That experience taught me so much. It taught me the value of being *really* present in the moment. It taught me how time can be bent, savored, and preserved – invested instead of just spent.

In July of 2012, he passed away – or as Amir would think of it, he transitioned from "in body" to "out of body." He's still checking in on me from time to time.

His journey through cancer and into the afterlife sent me into a deep obsession with health and vitality. I couldn't control what was happening with him, and it was so inconceivable to me that this healthy young man who played soccer and surfed almost every day could die of cancer at the age of 31.

I started wheat grassing, trying raw food cleanses, and drinking apple cider vinegar because I wanted to figure out how to biohack myself to live a long, healthy life.

And while my belief in myself improved and my obsession with my health grew, at 31, I found a secure job back at home building with a company that was beginning to grow again as the market began to recover. With my salary and bonuses as an Area Sales Manager, and with selling homes on the side, I was able to make enough to pay back $150,000 of debt I incurred during the time my income was abysmally low, and I started rebuilding my life.

A couple of months later, I met Igino, my soul mate and life partner. With him, it was all about the fun. It was boating on the weekends and playing tennis. We were very active, and we travelled. About eight months into dating, he moved back to the Bay Area from Orange County for a job opportunity, and for the next 14 months we continued with a long-distance relationship. We called it our long distance vacationship because we made it so fun.

Even though I was eating healthy and I was working out, I ended up in the ER one day. I actually thought I was having a heart attack at 31. It turns out that I was under a huge amount of stress and that manifested itself as an anxiety attack with chest pains.

That's when I realized that something had to change. Yes, my lifestyle was healthy, but this amount of stress wasn't sustainable.

◆

During the week, we would put 110% into our careers, getting up at 5:00 a.m. for yoga or spin class and being at work by 7:00 a.m. Often, I'd work

11 or 12 hours before meeting up with friends for dinner. Friday nights, I'd leave work at 5:00 p.m., catch the one-hour flight to the Bay Area from Orange County, and Igino and I would begin our weekend. Monday morning, I'd catch a 6:00 a.m. flight back to SoCal and be in the office before 8:00 a.m. Those three-night weekends become the building blocks of our long-distance vacationship.

I knew I wanted to be with him long-term, so we planned for me to move up to Northern California. After months of waiting, I finally had an opportunity for a job transfer with my company. It was ideal.

About a year before that, Igino had been diagnosed with cancer. It was a very treatable kind, and there's no reason to think he won't have an incredibly long healthy life, but it still is a scary thing to go through. I felt like lightning had hit twice. On top of that, his surgery was scheduled for the first day at my new job. I struggled with what to do. I didn't feel like I had a choice to ask for the day off when everything had already been planned. I was afraid that if I had to tell them that I needed to reschedule my opening meeting, that they would take that as me not being committed. My job and financial security were so important to me. Igino was the one who helped me make the decision, assuring me that I didn't need to be there, but to come after the surgery was done.

I sweated through the entire meeting because I was so scared and nervous on the inside about what was happening at the hospital. I drove from that meeting to the hospital in Stanford, crying the whole way. I kept thinking, "I don't ever want to be in this situation again where I don't feel like I have a choice." Did I have a choice? Absolutely. But I didn't really feel like I did. And I realized I was really trying to fit my life and the things that were important to me around my work. I just kept asking myself, "What is the way out? I don't know." I didn't know. But I knew I needed a way out.

As I drove, I realized that I'd been prioritizing jobs and money over my relationships, my passion, and my health. I vowed to myself that day that I would figure out a way to live in my passion professionally and personally. While I was waiting for him in post-op, I wrote down my passions – health, speaking, coaching, personal development, managing people, travel, organization, branding, and photography. I asked myself how I could combine those things to create a job that pays as good as it feels.

Not even one year later, I was introduced to network marketing. Coming from a very structured corporate world, I didn't take it seriously. I had used products of several different network marketing companies that friends or clients were involved in. I started a cleanse and a detox and was using nutritional products. I felt great, and my stress levels went down. It was amazing. My life wasn't necessarily changing, but my ability to cope with it was. That's when I started to explore the bigger picture.

I will say it has been a journey. I had to swallow a big ego, thinking that, "Oh, network marketing is great for stay-at-home moms and old ladies in glittery sweaters," but I'm used to working for a publicly traded company. I had to do a lot of research myself, and the more I researched, the more I realized that this was legit. Like anything else, there are people who are working really hard and are really successful, and there are people who dabble at it and say it doesn't work.

Real estate is the same way. There are a lot of people who get licensed in real estate and make no money because they're not actually doing it to have a successful career. But six months after using the product and diving into the opportunity, I started seeing all these women that were living this life I wanted. I believe that success leaves clues, and I wanted to know what they were doing. So I started filling my brain with all these possibilities. From a personal development standpoint, I hired a coach.

Then I started being very intentional about sharing products with people, and it started to pay.

In my fourth or fifth month of sharing, I earned $10,000. I thought, "This is insanity. This is my salary. Not my bonuses, but my salary. Wow." I'll definitely share more about that later in the book, but what I realized is that there was this other opportunity for me. It really fit everything I was looking for. I gave four months' notice at my other job and on January 1, 2015, I was able to go home and work for myself.

It was my first dip into entrepreneurship. Many call network marketing the gateway into entrepreneurship because it gives you the ability to start designing your day and your schedule. You can figure out where you're going to put your time and your energy. You have the total power to create the life you want, and the first step is realizing it's a real thing. When you realize it's available, you will go out and find the resources to do it.

WHERE I'M AT

That is my story. It has not been a straight path, but I am so grateful for where I am today. I have designed this life and this business I am in love with, while at the same time being a work in progress. I still have huge goals and things I want to change, and now I have the ability to do that.

My intention for this book is to give you the tools and resources that have taken me my entire life to realize. My goal is to give you a toolbelt you can use to design your life because you deserve to live a life that you are obsessed with. You deserve to live a life where you are excited to go to bed at night because you cannot wait to wake up in the morning. You have incredible opportunities in front of you, and I want to help you accomplish them.

MY PROMISE

This book is my gift to you, because I know what it feels like...

> To imagine there's more to life than working to live and then living for the weekends. To feel ungrateful for wanting more when you're achieving the goals you set and the goals you're not sure you want. For wondering if you're alone in feeling disconnected from the life you're living and the one you're sure is out there to be lived.

This book is for you if...

> You want to create a life of legacy instead of collecting a paycheck.
>
> You want to stop fantasizing about your dream life or business and start designing and living it.
>
> You want to understand why achievement feels empty or you're burned out or overwhelmed.
>
> You crave clarity and want to know where you're going and why.
>
> You are lost in a fog of what-ifs and need a compass to navigate your way out.

What else?

> You can start living today more connected, more joyous, more calm, and more purposeful.
>
> You will have incredible clarity on what aligns with your vision for your life and business.
>
> You will learn how to take focused action to move you toward that vision.
>
> You will identify where in your life you're out of alignment.

You will be able to do the things you want to do with so much less force and so much more flow.

You'll learn how to enjoy success when you achieve it.

You'll have the things that are important to you so much more easily.

You'll enjoy the challenges and growth on the journey.

You'll *actually* enjoy the journey.

Sound a bit too good to be true? I get it. It's the conditioning we've received in the story we've been sold that we need to *do* certain things to *have* certain things to *be* what we want. To feel the way we want.

It's life happening *to* us rather than happening *for* us. We are powerful creatures with the ability to create, though it's our responsibility and privilege to understand how to put that ability to work for the greater good of ourselves, our lives, and everything that we touch.

This book will allow you to *be*:

To *be* clear on what you want.

To *be* confident in embracing growth.

To *be* your best in your relationships.

To *be* your healthiest, most fit self, without dieting or killing yourself at the gym.

To *be* clear on a career or pursuit with purpose.

To *be* equipped with the tools and resources to create more joy, connection, and abundance in your life.

To *be* in action without the cycle of empty achievement.

To *be* able to release habits, beliefs, relationships, or attitudes that don't serve who you are becoming.

LET'S WRITE A BOOK

Just *be*.... what is it? Is it to be happy, be impactful, be confident, be in flow? It's that place, that nirvana, that we picture. It's our ideal state, our dream state, our flow state.

I've been talking about writing a book for years – actually, for decades, since I wrote my first short story 30 years ago and read it aloud in Mr. Spiker's fifth grade class. Ever since then, I was hooked on the idea of telling a story!

From years of reading fiction, I thought my first book would be a novel. But over the years, I've realized that reality is even more fascinating. The most riveting information of all are the tools that give us greater insight into ourselves and our ability to design our lives and create our own destinies.

I started a book two years ago on mind, body, and soul wellness (nutrition + mindset) for women trying to get pregnant or who were pregnant. The more research I did and the more I wrote, the more I felt like I needed to research. And I talked a lot more about writing it than actually writing it. I second-guessed and third-guessed myself on why I didn't know enough or wasn't credentialed enough.

Last year, my husband asked me, "What are you waiting for?" I had a lot of excuses, but in my gut, I knew the book I wanted to write would pull me instead of requiring me to *push*. He suggested I write the book I was already an expert on, the one that I didn't need a Ph.D. to prove or dozens of interviews to complete.

It seemed ridiculously obvious, so much so that I hadn't seen it myself. I had that kind of realization that you know if you follow the pull, everything will change. And when he told me, "If you just sat down and committed to this, you could write this book in a week," it didn't actually sound that crazy. I'd been writing the book in my head (and in part, on social media posts and blogs) for the past several years.

I had to get out of my house in the same way I got out of my head, so I sat in the public library pulling together snippets that I'd written over the years, watching the thread of them come together. My phone was on airplane mode and the internet browser was closed. I was *free* writing all of the messages, lessons, pains, and triumphs I've experienced and the simple lessons I learned to get through it all. And it began to write itself.

When I gave up the control and focus on the *being* of my writer self, my self that is the expert of my own life and of the lessons I've learned, was able to take over. My self knows what I've gone through, not just where I am and the clarity of where I'm going, but the frustration, pain, and challenges I can save someone else from experiencing when I share my story.

The remaining 50% took me another two years. Though the realization that led to this book was so simple, as I began to detail out the way it could be used as a tool to identify what you want, then to design a life around that, I wanted to put it into purposeful practice myself. And so I did.

In the past 24 months, I became my own beta project using the BE Formula. I've co-founded a second business I'm obsessed with, launched a top-ranked podcast I feel I was made to create, had my second baby in the most magical home birth experience, traveled for nearly 20% of the year, and wrote a curriculum for a course during a car ride.

It sounds like I'm doing more, but I promise you, the resistance and effort has been less. And I'm so excited to share with you how.

And now you're sitting here reading this, which means I've allowed this book to live where it belongs, on paper, where it can benefit others instead of just in my head.

If you've got a dream that is pulling you, stop fighting it. Stop talking about it. Start *being* it.

CHAPTER 2

What Are You Waiting For?

*"The biggest adventure you can ever take is
to live the life of your dreams."*

– OPRAH WINFREY

BUT REALLY?

The *right time* or perfect opportunity to finally quit that job you aren't in love with or start that dream business you fantasize about? The book you'll write? The blog-worthy trip you'll finally take or the relationships you'll attract? It's the stuff that vision boards are made of. It's the New Year's Resolutions that get recycled year after year after year.

Are you waiting to start your dream business until after you are more successful in your current job? To take the trip once you have the credit card paid off? To start wearing that outfit and feeling confident after you've hit your goal weight? It's seducing to think so.

Why are you waiting to reward yourself with what you want until after you've punished yourself to get there?

What class do you need to take? What book do you need to read? How much overtime do you need to work? What skills must you first master? And how many gym visits (and missed desserts) must happen?

Or perhaps, you have prepared a well-organized list of action steps and accomplishments that you'd first need to do or have in order to get to the final goal. Or *after* a certain amount of time passes or someone else creates the resources, space, or money for you to finally make it happen.

The truth? You have to take your own opportunity and *make* it perfect for you. And what is that opportunity? It's how you would be, how you would live, how you would feel... when there are no excuses.

It's what you would be doing if money wasn't a concern. It's how you would feel if you didn't *need* coffee or sugar fixes or had no reason to not go take that belly dance class. It's the places you would go if your biggest concern about vacation was what to pack.

Or worst case, we're waiting on luck, chance, the universe, or the idea that just "keep on keeping on" will eventually, at some undefined point in the future, get us there.

But really?

Waiting for the perfect opportunity is like waiting to win a lottery you haven't bought a ticket for. The perfect time will never come if life is happening *to* you and not *for* you.

How often do *you* do this? You say, "When I have *this*... then I can do *that*... and I'll finally *be this!*

Who do you want to become? When will you begin living a life you design? When will you be the person deserving of it? And who are you now?

WHY YOU NEED IT

My husband once told me, "Do what you need to be happy, because when you are happy, you can do anything!" It's become my mantra.

The question of how to be happy is one that endless books have been written about and millions of dollars have been spent in therapy, coaching, at retreats, and personal development workshops to come up with the perfect answer. And while happiness isn't a destination, it's the one emotion we as humans desire to feel or be.

How do you want to be? To show up each day? What are the feelings you want to experience?

Why is the BE formula so important?

Before any great invention or achievement, someone *saw* it first. They were required to *be* it before they did it or had it. They may not have had the exact *how*, but they had an idea of the end goal. They didn't see each step, but they had faith as they took the first one. And it's the same thing as you *become* the person you are meant to be as you design the life you were meant to live.

What is the secret of those people we want to be like? The secrets of those elusive happy people or the people who are successful while enjoying the success? There are so many different strategies out there promising success if you just give ten times the effort or become so efficient and leveraged you can do it all in a four-hour work week. But what's right? Different strategies are just different routes to the destination of where you want to be. We often obsess over what to do to be happy and successful or how to do it. But at the center of it all is *why* we want to do it.

There's a reason that dream keeps popping up. When your mind wanders, it goes there. It was put into your head, your heart, and your life for a reason. You were gifted it, and if you don't do something about it, it's going to take up residence somewhere else. And it will be the one that got away in a more profound sense than any relationship, because you had the ability to bring it to life, and you also have the power to define it as a reality or as a dream.

Don't let it get away. And the dream killers? They are excuses, obligation, comparison, waiting, and self-doubt.

So what do you want out of this life?

You've heard those deathbed stories. No one talks about wishing they had worked more hours or saved more money. They wish they would have *been* more – more happy, more connected to their loved ones, more free with their time, more compassionate with their dreams.

And *why*? Why is it so important to not stay where we are today? Why is it so important to realize our dreams? Because on the other side of those things we need to do, of those things we'll be able to have, lies what we'll be able to be. Happy. Free. Confident. Connected. Healthy. Impactful.

You just *know* that when you're sitting right in the middle of that goal life, you'll feel all the feelings. The really juicy, good ones, the ones we listen to our favorite song to get a hint of, that we watch that favorite movie to feel part of – joy, abundance, purpose, and fun!

What's stopping us? From getting on with – or *starting* – your life, where you have complete freedom? Where you can do what you want, when you want, and with whom you want. Where you can have your own voice and make your own choices to what you feel called to do, not obligated to do. Do you ever feel like you're constantly struggling against expectations, social norms, commitments, and even yourself?

What's keeping you from that life? A lack of something? A lack of time, resources, education, confidence, support?

How often are we waiting for things to change? Waiting for a different season, waiting for the bonus to take the trip, waiting for the kids to graduate, waiting for our partner to change?

Why do we give all of the power to things we may not control? Why don't we focus on what we have *total* control over? Ourselves — and the reality that we *can* design a life not only worth loving, but one that we can be ourselves in.

We've heard it before.

You are capable of anything you set your mind to! Whatever is going on in your life right now, you have the grit, the resourcefulness, and the power to overcome it and to thrive! You are uniquely you, with gifts and talents no one else has. You're the only one who is an expert on your life!

And we know it. Or we want to believe it. But in between feeling inspired and brave for moments or even hours, we have LONG stretches where we are sure that THING that will give us the key to it all is just out there. On another podcast, an e-mail list or in a course we're afraid not to sign up for.

You don't need the dream guy, the right book, the killer outfit, or the ideal job to break through where you're currently at to create that place you know you deserve to be. So stop waiting for a better day, the beginning of the month, after whatever crisis is happening is over to reach within and release your happiest self. Timing will never be perfect, but there's no better time to move your life forward than today!

And you're reading this, so the path awaits. Are you ready to take a step forward?

WHAT YOU CAN DO WITH THIS

The Be Formula is a way to answer the question: What do you *really* want?

Who do you want to *become*? How do I take focused action?

How do I know I'm on the right path? What do I want *out* of this life?

And to find the answer to this question:

If my life were more _____, what would it look like?

STOP FANTASIZING, START LIVING

How many of you couldn't wait to finish high school and go to college? To get on with your life where you'd have complete freedom? Where you could do what you wanted, when you wanted, and with whom you wanted. Where you could have your own voice and make your own choices. Did you ever feel like you were constantly struggling against expectations, social norms, your parents, and even yourself?

I remember feeling that same way my senior year of high school.

For most of my senior year, I told myself, "When I have my diploma, I'll be an adult, and I'll finally *be free* (to date who I want, wear what I want, work where I want)."

I couldn't *wait* for that final bell to ring. To shake the principal's hand. For the senior party to end. Graduation night held double the excitement for me because I planned to move away from home the very next morning. Everything I owned was packed up and crammed inside my 1988 Chevy Beretta in anticipation of *tomorrow*. I felt euphoric knowing I was *done*! My life was finally about to begin.

You see, high school was tough. I'm sure it was for you too. Maybe you faced academic difficulties, social troubles, parental growing pains, or internally focused heartache. Maybe at some point, you've even battled them all.

There's often a romanticism that surrounds our senior year of high school as the excitement that college is closer than ever – the nostalgia of four years of great memories and fun coming to a close or feeling pressure to squeeze every last bit of adolescent fun. That, however, wasn't my experience.

My parents and I went head to head over disagreements about my high school boyfriend, so often that I spent a good part of my senior year grounded, engrossed in conflict, or recovering from our most recent argument. It escalated to the point that I finished the school year living with my grandmother.

That should have been my saving grace, except for the fact that once I finished with homework each day, she put me to work doing manual labor for her business. Neither environment allowed me any sense of independence, something all my friends seemed to have. I counted down the days until graduation.

Nothing sounded better than moving on to all of the freedom that college represented. I was only going to be an hour from my parents, but in terms of freedom, it felt like I was crossing an entire ocean. I vowed that *everything* was going to be different. And guess what?

I didn't get the perfect roommate. Or the perfect job. Or straight As all year. And because freshman year didn't play out *exactly* as I dreamed it would, I felt disappointed, like I'd let myself down.

How often do you say, "When I *have* this accomplishment, this promotion, this recognition, then I can *do* that, and I'll finally *be* this. When I have my coaching certification, I'll take coaching clients and I'll be confident in my value. When I get to my goal weight, I'll be able to fit into my skinny jeans and I'll love my body. Or when I replace my income with my side hustle, I'll be able to leave my job and I'll feel free.

As we make decisions about everything we do, we will learn to recognize what moves us closer to our BE state and choose those, and also learn to recognize what moves us further from our BE state, and choose those less or eliminate them all together.

The Institute for Integrative Nutrition, where I received my certification in Holistic Health and Integrative Nutrition, teaches a concept called "crowding out." Instead of depriving ourselves, we are taught to focus more on the goodness of what makes us healthy and happy. And in this book, we will focus on choosing the things that allow us to be more – more in our ideal state, more in the flow of feeling one with our best self.

Being is not about *being* perfectly. Trying to be perfect is unrealistic and puts us in a state of doing. And let's face it, you've tried it before, and it didn't work. In the following pages, you will learn how *being* is the way, not the result, to designing a life and business you love! *being* is the means.

CHAPTER 3

The Cycle Of Empty Achievement

*"Unhappiness is not knowing what we want
and killing ourselves to get it."*

— DON HERALD

At 26, life was perfect — from the outside. I had just moved into the house of my dreams, customized to my every specification, with panoramic views of the city. I was winning awards at work and earning more than a quarter of a million dollars per year. I was driving a luxury car after spending part of my childhood in a single parent household below the poverty line. I had everything I wanted when I thought about success and even more.

And I was miserable. I asked myself repeatedly, "Is this it?" I felt like something was wrong with me. I fantasized about giving up everything to travel. I felt trapped by my mortgage, my relationship, my job. How dare I be so ungrateful?

On paper, everything looked incredible. But we don't live on paper. We are three-dimensional humans with hearts that yearn and souls that only get louder when we lie to ourselves.

When you get what you thought you wanted and it's hollow, what do you do? Fill the hollow space, that seemed to be the obvious answer. So I searched for everything I could to inject more joy into my life.

I hired a life coach and proceeded to tell her the mapped-out success trajectory of my life. She listened politely for 10 minutes, then asked me, "What do you *really* want?" I completely broke down and sobbed my eyes out. When people had been asking me my work or income goals or what I was *doing* over the past five years, no one really asked what I *wanted* – at a soul level.

And the answers spewed forth as fast as my tears. I wanted to take acting classes, I wanted to dance, to take circus classes, to volunteer, to travel. I wanted to BE creative, to BE impactful, to BE experiencing all of the joy that life had to offer.

I didn't quit my job or sell all of my worldly possessions (though I considered it often), but I made the decision to start injecting joy and purpose into my life. I began to volunteer, giving my time as a tutor to a foster pre-teen and organizing clothing drives for the local homeless shelter. And I felt a little bit better, at least in the moments I was *being* impactful.

And I signed up for a photography class, a circus school class, and a theater class. And I felt better in the moments I was there or practicing or was *being* creative.

And I traveled! I actually took time off (after years of not taking vacations) and that year, went to Thailand, Belize, Hawaii, and the Caribbean. The travel was lovely, but I'd find myself spending the last half of the trip stressing out about being back to work. And when I got back, I'd be daydreaming and planning the next trip. I enjoyed the escape of planning as much as the trip itself (and sometimes more, because my vision was usually superior to the reality).

But the joy didn't last long after I left the vacation spot or volunteering hours. And each time I did it again, the result was slightly less satisfying, like taking that first bite of a dessert and realizing each bite after wasn't quite as good but eating it anyway in the hopes it would be.

I was living a life of neutrality and living *for* the staccato moments of joy or impact or creativity. I knew there must be more.

Do you ever think your life looks really good when someone else is describing it, yet you can't figure out why you don't feel fulfilled or happy?

I used to write down all the things that were going well. It wasn't exactly a gratitude list; it was more my way of convincing myself that the things other people told me were important really were.

And I felt like a fraud because I knew my life was good, but I felt like there was so much more just beyond reach. More happiness, more fulfillment, more joy, more fun, more purpose. And when I met people that seemed to have it, I wonder if they *really* did, or if they also were putting up a facade.

There's no title or step up a ladder that will ever give us the life that our inner child is begging us for. Sometimes those people who seem really, really happy might really be, not because their life is perfect, but because they are living for what they believe in.

If you're dreading Monday morning like I used to or doubting there really are people that are excited for their workday to begin, I'd love to share what totally changed my life.

THE CYCLE OF EMPTY ACHIEVEMENT

How often do *you* do this? You say, "When I have *this*... then I can do *that*... and I'll finally be *this!*"

When I get that promotion, I'll be able to make enough to pay my bills, travel, and make my own schedule. And I'll be successful!

When I get to my goal weight, I'll be able to wear a swimsuit and feel confident!

Sometimes, I got *exactly* what I wanted. That something that was so crucial to unlocking my happiness, confidence, or sense of wholeness.

Like being awarded Salesperson of the Year. Having my article published. Buying my first house.

And you know what? It never felt like I imagined it would. I wasn't any happier, more confident, or more complete. So I'd achieve the goal and experience a day of feeling fulfilled and happy.

Then I'd start the process all over. I'd set another goal to obtain or achieve something. I made vision boards. I made list after list of goals and to-dos. There weren't enough hours left in the day to sleep with everything I needed to do!

Ironically, I'd add "sleep more" to my list of goals year after year. Not surprisingly, I never did reach that goal.

I became a master at checking to-haves and to-dos off my list, but I never could quite grasp that elusive *feeling* of accomplishment that I expected. Or if I did feel it, it was short-lived.

I realized this cycle of achievement had been going on in my life for years – since I was a kid, when I consciously realized that getting attention felt really good. As I had an irrational fear of getting in trouble for fear that it would mean the people I'd love would leave, the attention I sought out was validation for achievement.

The grind leads to burnout and overwhelm. We have the illusion it'll get us to our goals and dreams, but it comes at the cost of self-care, joy, and taking the time to be conscious of how we are showing up. We're on a path that will never lead to real fulfillment.

So how do we get to enjoy the success we are lusting after? Or stop burning ourselves out for the pursuit of something that isn't even clear? What's it worth if we aren't pausing to savor or enjoy? If we wake up 20 years down the road and we wake up not feeling fulfilled?

But there is hope.

Six years ago, I was at a great job with an impressive title, getting a promotion I realized I didn't want. I was trying to squeeze every moment out of every weekend with the hope staying busy would keep me from realizing I wasn't really happy.

I can't believe how much can change in a few years. I quit my corporate career, started my own business, had two babies, sold our condo, built our dream house, and began following passions that were just entries in the bucket list a few years ago.

The saying "Create a life you don't need a vacation from" really hit home for me. If you're not exactly where you want to be, don't be frustrated. You *can* change it. You can create your day. It's not inspirational hype.

You're about to figure out the coordinates of what that future looks like and plug them into your GPS. It's time to get in the driver's seat of your life and hit the road to your future! And to really, finally, enjoy that journey.

WORSE, LIVING IN SURVIVAL MODE

There is something worse than setting goals you work blindly toward, even when crossing the finish line brings you little joy. It's reaching a point where you stop setting goals, where you stop moving forward.

Perhaps you've told yourself, "I don't want to set a goal because I won't achieve it." Or you've realized that setting the goal becomes more important than the goal itself.

Going from Point A to Point B without purpose can rob our lives of the magic of the vision seeking to express itself. BE receptive to the vision.

Why are goals and progress important?

"Don't ever change." It's the phrase written in numerous high school yearbooks and a curse to anyone who follows it.

Why? Because as humans, we are changing as much as the world around us is, as much as the body we live within is. And if we don't change, if we stay stagnant, we begin to feel stuck – or as the world moves around us, that we're even going backward.

Change may be a given, but progress is a choice.

What goals or resolutions did you make at the beginning of the year? For many people, they didn't set goals because they know they won't move forward and want to avoid disappointment. For many that did set goals, they've already given up.

Don't give up on moving forward, on making progress. You don't need a new year to improve your mindset, your health, your relationships, your finances, and your contribution.

"Progress equals happiness. Even if you're not where you want to be yet. If you're on the road, if you're improving, if you're making progress."

— TONY ROBBINS

CHAPTER 4

Just Being

"When YOU begin to change, everything will begin to change around you. If you want things to get better, YOU have got to get better."

– JIM ROHN

There have been times in my life that I've *really* struggled. Ten years ago, I lost everything – my income, my home, my peace of mind.

My boyfriend was fighting Stage IV cancer. I remember sitting next to his hospital bed during his weekly chemotherapy, afraid that if I left, his health might take a turn for the worse – but afraid of losing my job if I missed any more work.

Happiness should have been non-existent, but surprisingly, I recall moments of intense joy, laughter, and fun, moments where I wasn't thinking about my overdrawn bank account or worrying about my job.

I lived in the moment. Finding beauty in the mundane. Laughing at situations that could have easily evoked tears. Wringing out every bit of happiness by just *being*. *Being present was the only thing that mattered because the future was so uncertain.*

41

I didn't understand what I was doing to be able to be present and joyful in the midst of life falling down around me. Those moments were pinpoints of light when I was in the midst of such darkness.

Over the past 10 years, I've been *consciously* searching for the answer to finding the formula to BE. In books, with coaches (and therapists), in conversations with the happy (and unhappy). Everything and everyone promised the next *thing* that would result in less confusion, more clarity, more ease, and of course, with it more success, happiness, better health, money (and yes, even better sex)! And many things helped when I was consistent. They helped me grow. They were a piece of the recipe. But it wasn't the *thing*.

On a call with a business coach a few years ago, he had me do a visualization that shifted *everything*. Suddenly, all of those pieces of self-help and self-development and challenges and belief and times of ease and times of anxiety *all* came together.

I realized my path had been a big puzzle.... I had all of the pieces there, but they weren't connected in a way that showed me the big picture. All those years, I'd kept looking at the pieces, feeling like I should be able to put them together, but never could. So I just kept moving them around in busy-ness but not in clarity.

And suddenly, I could see it.

THE SECRET TO HAVING IT ALL

For more than a decade of personal development, coaching, attending retreats, having accountability partners, and immersing myself into ways to optimize my life to be the happiest, most successful, most passionate version of me, this tool that I'm sharing with you today is the key that's unlocked really living everything I've learned.

In 2017, I crossed off a big bucket list item when I had the opportunity to speak at TEDx, and this key, this realization, this formula, was my message. I wholeheartedly believe that if you put this simple concept into practice, it can radically change your life like it changed mine. It's the foundation to building a life you'll love. I call it the BE Formula.

The BE Formula is a way to answer the question of what we really want. The key question to ask is, "How do I want to be?"

Once you get clear on the qualities you want to embody, ask yourself "If my life were more _____, what would that look like?"

Joyous, connected, and abundant is my personal ideal BE State, but yours will be different. How do you want to be? How do you take focused action in that state of *being*? How do you know if you're on the right path? What do you want out of life this year, this week, even this day?

What are you waiting for to design your dream life or business? If you're reading this, you have a desire to make a change. You want to improve something. You understand that good can be the enemy of great. It doesn't mean that you don't like your life now, but it means that you have this feeling in your soul that you're meant for more. As author and thought leader Peta Kelly said, "Be the most grateful yet unsatisfied person you've ever met."

So what are you waiting for? Are you waiting to reward yourself with what you enjoy or crave, but first punishing yourself to get there? What class do you need to take? What book do you need to read? How much over-time do you need to work? What skills do you need to master? Or you're indulging in temporary rewards like retail therapy or scrolling social media that get you no closer to the state of being you really crave.

Or maybe you're like me, you're a list maker, with a well-organized list of action steps and goals that you first need to do in order to get to your final goal.

This opportunity is really to figure out how you want to be, how you want to live, how you want to feel.

How often do we get what we want? Because sometimes we do. We achieve the goal, that *something* that was supposed to be so crucial to us feeling happy or confident or just feeling whole. But I know for me, it rarely felt like I imagined it would. It was not the fix-all. I wasn't necessarily happier, I wasn't more confident, I wasn't more complete. Or if I felt that way, it was short-lived.

So I'd start the process over. I'd set another goal and I'd make another vision board or to-do list. I became a master at checking off the to-haves and to-dos off my list, but I never felt that feeling of accomplishment and wholeness that I expected because I was focusing on the *have* and the *do* in order to BE.

It took me 37 years to uncover the secret to having it all, and I would love to save you time. Imagine all the things you've dreamed about having or achieving, the things that you've pinned on Pinterest or saved on Instagram or put on vision boards. The things that you put into sentences like, "When I have this, I can." Maybe it's the relationship or the car or the vacation, or it's the idea of what success looks like. What have you dreamed of having or achieving?

Now, imagine that you have them, that you've accomplished the goal. You've got those things that you thought were so important. How does it feel? What are you able to do, now that you've achieved it? Maybe it's sitting on the Amalfi Coast, on a terrace outside, sipping rose, being totally present to everything you're experiencing. Maybe you're cruising down a coastal highway in the Tesla car you bought with the bonus you got from your promotion, feeling free.

But how does it feel to be able to do the things you've dreamed of doing, when you *have* affirmations and your *do* statements become a reality?

Now that you have all those things you want, and you're able to do all the things you've been waiting for, what does that allow you to BE? Are you more confident with that promotion? Do you walk down the hallway at work with your head held high? Are you immersed in gratitude at your body for health and strength when you finished that 30-day yoga challenge you signed up for? What are those qualities – confident, grateful, generous, happy? What are you free to be when you've got the things you want and you're able to do the things that you like? Who do you show up as?

What would happen if you became those traits right now – more confident, more grateful, more generous, more connected, more happy? How would you walk out of your house? How would your habits change? How would you look in the mirror? How would you treat others? What would it feel like to be that person? What's stopping you from being that person right now? It's not a physical thing. It's not an accomplishment. It's not a relationship. It's not a title.

The real secret is that it's not about having it all. In fact, it's not about having at all. *Being* is the way, not the result. That "ideal life" isn't outside of you, it starts within you.

You could have everything and do everything with so much more ease and flow, if you choose to be that person now. Instead of *having* in order to *be*, *be* in order to *have*.

Being is a state of mind. It's a decision we make every day, every moment, to be in a "BE" state, not in a "do" state. When we're in the "do" state, we're constantly thinking, "I should be doing this. I should be doing that." We're called by obligation and lost in a world of "should" dos."

When we make a goal because we think it'll help us get somewhere, because it sounds good on a resume, or because someone told us that we should, we're creating a GPS coordinate based upon a do. If we get off track, we do have the end goal to bring us back. But what happens when we shift priorities or we shift focus, and suddenly that goal seems like a grind? You're no longer called to it, but you've committed to it and you don't want to feel like a quitter by not going after it. What if instead you asked yourself, "Does achieving this allow me to experience my ideal BE state?"

If you feel like you're a master at checking to to-haves and to-dos off your list, but never can quite grasp the *feeling* of happiness you expect, the BE Formula is for you!

IT'S NOT ABOUT HAVING AT ALL, IT'S ABOUT BELIEVING YOU ALREADY DO

You can **have** everything and **do** everything with so much more ease and flow if you choose to **BE** that person now.

Be. Do. Have.

Being is a state of mind. It's a decision you make each day. Each moment. You must be in a BE state, not a DO state.

When you are in a do state, you think, "I *should* do this." and "I *should* do that." Stop *should*-ing all over yourself! After all, you are a human *being*, not a human DOING.

46

BE isn't about wishing you were someone else. It's about *becoming* your best self.

CHOOSE TO BE THAT PERSON NOW

Stop working so hard on your to-have and to-do lists, because they are never-ending.

The real task? Create a *to-be list.*

What are the qualities you want to BE? Define them. Be clear on what they are.

To BE generous.

Do things that resonate with generosity.

To BE happy.

Do things that make you happy.

To BE helpful.

Help someone in need.

When you encounter a challenging situation, ask yourself what YOU five or 10 years from now would do. The you who is heard, impactful, and confident. The you who would consciously decide to **BE** your best self again and again. Not perfectly, but in a way that moves you forward.

Suddenly, you stop striving, and you start *being.*

If you're striving for a goal that takes one, five, 10 years (or even longer) to achieve, but aren't allowing yourself to *feel* happy or fulfilled until you reach it, how can you hope to live and feel happy in the moment?

What is a life? It's a lot of years, days, and moments strung together. You choose. The moment that creates the day. The days that create the year. The years that create the life.

And what's the goal in it all? To live a life of happiness, of purpose, a life where you are uniquely you. A life where your voice is not only heard but is a ripple that impacts others. Other people can *have* the same things. They can even *do* the same things. But they can never BE you.

"Sure it's been done before. But not by you. And not for us."

– SETH GODIN

◆

Below are three exercises you can do to immediately start incorporating your BE state into designing the life and the business that you love.

TOOLS FOR *BEING*, #1
THE BE LIST

Your first step is to first create a BE list. Write down the qualities you want to be. Define them. Be clear on what they are.

Write down 20 qualities you'd love to BE (Example: joyous, connected, calm, present, grateful):

_____

_____

_____

_____

Next, circle your top 10.

Now, underline your top five.

Finally, what are the three qualities that you want to BE? That reso-nate with your soul? That living in would mean living in your best self, living your best life. Write them below.

Those three qualities will be your ideal BE state and your affirmation.

My ideal BE state is:

_____

_____

_____

What does that feel like? Define what each of those words mean to you.

_____

_____

_____

And what do you do with these three qualities? Every day I write down on my daily intention sheet the intention I have for being. It's the first thing I do before I ask myself what I want to accomplish. What are my goals? It's my intention for being.

Affirmation: I am _____, _____ and _____.

Example:

Affirmation: I am abundant, relaxed, and joyous.
OR
Affirmation: I am focused, feeling, and in flow.

◆

TOOLS FOR *BEING*, #2
MAKING TIME TO BE

Think about the times of day when you're the most stressed out or the furthest from your ideal BE state. It might be 6:00 a.m. when you're wanting to hit snooze, at 2:00 p.m. during the mid-afternoon slump, or at 7:00 p.m. when you're making the decision between a glass (or second glass) of wine and Netflix or finishing that creative project.

Pick three or four times of day.

Set an alarm in your phone for those times.

Title it: BE _____, _____, _____.

Set music to it – it's hard to feel any great qualities when triggered by an aggressive alarm! Select a song that assists you in feeling your best!

When your alarm goes off, spend a minute (or the entire song) focusing on your breath and feeling *in* to the emotions! Dance parties are also highly encouraged!

◆

In my personal life, those qualities are relaxed, abundant, and joyous. In my work life, it's focused and feeling in the flow. I show up with a different vibrational energy depending on whether I'm showing up for my child or for my team. Throughout the day, I do check-ins with myself, in addition to my alarms, to see if I need to change up how I'm being or what

TIP Tell others around you how you want to be! Your team, whether your family or your work team, is there to help you grow! Have them encourage you when you're *being*.

I'm doing. I ask myself, "How am I feeling right now? Is what I'm doing now taking away from that ideal BE state? What could I do to feel more relaxed or more abundant or more joyous?"

Sometimes it's just a quick meditation or it's walking outside to feel more connected. Sometimes it's rescheduling a commitment if I feel like I'm rushed and I'm hurrying through things and I'm not in my ideal state. It might be writing down gratitudes on a Post-it and putting it in front of me on the window in front of my computer. The answer is very rarely ever found on my phone or social media. In fact, often those totally take me out of that ideal BE state.

When your BE state become your GPS coordinates, it helps you map out the actions, the to-do, with so much more flow and so much less obligation. But let's be real. This doesn't mean you're never going to do something that doesn't feel great, because growth is uncomfortable. Growth is challenging. But it also means you're going to clear so much noise out of your head, commitments out of your schedule that don't serve you, and even relationships out of your life that might be holding you back from being your best self.

◆

YOUR GPS COORDINATES

Create BE goals as specific as GPS coordinates and you'll never be lost. First, what do we need to know?

WHO do you want to BE?

HOW do you want to BE?

WHAT do you want?

WHO do you want to BEcome?

When you put your destination in the GPS, your path is laid out for you. And if you detour, it'll create a route to get you back on track. For years, I thought of my goals as these coordinates, and it was helpful. The problem was that my goals often changed based upon opportunities or where I felt my passion was shifting.

Instead, our BE is the GPS coordinates. Our goal locations will continue to shift, but our BE state will keep us on track. In fact, it'll assist us in deciding if we even care about getting to that goal, if that goal really aligns with where we want to go and who we want to BE.

Ask yourself: if my life were more _____, what would it look like? What's my intention for *Being*?

How would a life *fully* true to yourself, one that is unreasonably joyful and purposeful, look different from the one you are leading now?

What's that life look like that is both driven and guided (and grounded). What is the BE that guides us?

Our BE state is the GPS coordinates as well as the navigation. When we get on track, we have the navigation system to reroute us. But it only works if we program in the correct destination and if we listen to it as it navigates the way.

Clarity isn't about seeing the entire path, but it's about being able to feel it when you aren't on it. And when you are.

Write it out! This book isn't just to inspire you, it's to empower you to *design* your life. And every great design starts with putting the pen (or pencil) to paper! So get specific!

TOOLS FOR *BEING*, #3
ALIGNING YOUR GOALS
WITH YOUR BE STATE

1. Write down your ideal BE state, the qualities you want to be each day, the feelings you want to live in.

    _____

    _____

    _____

2. Look at your current goals. How do those align with your ideal BE state? Are there goals you want to release and let go? Are there things you have been called to do but you haven't allowed yourself to do them? Write down your goals.

    _____

    _____

    _____

One of my former goals for years was to be a division president in my real estate career. It was the ultimate goal within my industry that came with a sizable compensation package, hundreds of employees, paid trips, and an impressive title. The decisions I made for years in my career and the times my actions following a "should" were serving this goal, even when it felt out of alignment with me.

But had I asked myself if that really aligned with my BE state, the answer would have been easily clear. I knew the time away from family wouldn't make me feel connected. That the stress at that level wouldn't make me feel joyous. And the demands on my time wouldn't feel abundant.

LIFE GOALS: BUSINESS AND PERSONAL

Five-Year Goals:

_____

_____

_____

_____

One-Year Goals:

_____

_____

_____

_____

90-Day Goals:

_____

_____

_____

_____

30-Day Goals:

_____

_____

_____

_____

TOOLS FOR *BEING*, #4
ROADBLOCKS

How would you spend your time if you were living in your BE state? What would you be doing? With whom? And where? What would you be wearing? How would you feel about it?

_____

_____

_____

_____

ROADBLOCKS

While it's a great start to write what we want, we also need to realize what could distract us.

What is currently keeping me from *being* that person now?

Write down potential roadblocks:

_____

_____

_____

_____

TOOLS FOR *BEING*, #5
COMMITTING TO YOUR BE STATE

Write your current commitments below. This could be monthly meetings, classes, or social gatherings.

RECURRING COMMITMENTS

_____

_____

_____

SOCIAL COMMITMENTS

_____

_____

_____

OTHER COMMITMENTS

_____

_____

_____

Which of these align with your BE state? Are you doing some out of obligation, knowing it'll drain your energy? Are you spending time with people who don't light you up because you're afraid to say no?

With your BE state as the coordinate, which of these would you release?

BE willing to say no! Every time you say yes to something, you say no to something else. When you do something that doesn't align with your BE state or goals, you're sending yourself a message that other people's priorities are more important than yours.

 If you're torn on an obligation due to making a commitment or because you feel you'll let someone down, imagine going to bed and that commitment being gone. When you wake up, are you relieved or are you regretful? There is your answer!

Commitments to Release:

_____

_____

_____

_____

_____

_____

_____

How does that feel? Can you breathe easier with more space on your calendar in your life? Knowing you're going in the direction of your ideal BE state and protecting your energy (and calendar) from obligations that don't serve it?

CHAPTER 5

What It Really Takes

"There's No Such Thing As Failure, Only Feedback."
– KARI KEATING

GIVING UP CONTROL

Ever been told you're a control freak? I have! What's even harder than admitting it is overcoming it. And when you're in control of your control, it's *impossible* to be living in your BE state or to be intentional about creating the conditions that allow you to BE.

For the few weeks after having my baby girl, I thought a lot about my birth experience and how different it was from my first. The difference? One was a medicated hospital birth and the second one was a natural home birth, but at the core, it came down to control. Releasing control changed everything and actually created the experience I wanted to have the first time.

The definition of control is a power to influence or direct people's behavior or the course of events. Control can look like taking on too much, trying to do it all, saying things like, "Oh don't worry, I can handle it." It can look like not asking for help, thinking vulnerability is a weakness, or being disappointed when someone doesn't act the way that you think they should or that you want them to.

Does any of that hit home? For me, those were all things that I said or thought for most of my life.

Over the past couple of years as I've learned to release control, it's incredible how much more I am able to live in my BE state and how much more effortless my life can be (even with kids)! But it takes effort to be effortless.

The reality is that we can't control it all. We can't always be right. And not needing anybody, not needing anything, doesn't allow us to be our most powerful, impactful, and strongest selves. And what is control's real motivator? Fear.

Fear stands for False Evidence Appearing Real, and that's what is happening when we try to control it all. When we are trying to be in control, we're really dealing with fear – thinking, "If someone can do this better, I'm not needed." Or if I have the bandwidth to focus on what I am meant to be doing instead of just being busy by controlling everything, I might actually experience the success I'm really afraid of. Control is about fear, restriction, and limits.

An acquaintance once told me I never seemed to be afraid and asked how I got past fear. How did I learn to relinquish control and relinquish fear? My response was, "First, I still feel fear. But I've learned to give up control. It was seeing that things don't crash and burn."

But there's really a simple answer to this. The way to give up control is to replace it with intention.

In the past, when I would "give up control," I wouldn't set someone else up for success. I would set them up for failure. I didn't realize this or consciously plan to do so, but I was subconsciously doing it so that I could be right, so I could be needed. It would justify my control of the situation or the story that I had to have control. I was like a dog chasing its tail.

What happened when I really learned to give up control? When I set an intention to prepare that person or that situation for success, where I actually wasn't needed? I saw that things were fine. They may not have been done the exact way that I wanted them to, but guess what? That's okay. The result was that it freed me up to do the things I was meant to do, and in the process, become the person I was meant to be.

Understand, control does not mean organized. It does not always mean perfect. In fact, often we're controlling our lives through chaos. We are addicted to it. We are using the overwhelm as an excuse to not move forward, controlling the outcome by never taking the first step.

In business, I would hear highly successful content creators say you need to plan out your social media if you want to be consistent. But that felt controlled. And I would say, "No, I'm only going to post when I feel like it." And then it would be 9:00 a.m. Monday and I'd be scrambling to come up with something halfhearted and not authentically me. The reality was that bringing value to my audience, to impact more people, required me being more consistent in showing up.

So what did giving up control look like? I asked myself, "How can I be intentional by planning it out? How can I feel it? How can I be intentional in feeling before I write out content?"

When I decided to stop controlling the chaos, a formula emerged for me to creating soul driven, purposeful content that actually sounded like me (the me who would attract clients and customers I wanted to collaborate with or serve). I start with meditation to clear the brain, then movement to get my body firing, and then reading or listening to a podcast to inspire me. When I do those things, it sets me up to create content that is authentically me. It's when the best ideas and thoughts come to me. And it's when my audience responds.

And when you add other people to the equation, it only *gets more* complicated and messy because they have their own fears and need of control.

When I hired one of my first assistants, I was always busy and scrambling to delegate to her! I wouldn't have her tasks mapped out for her because I was so busy dealing with one fire or another. **Busy is a word that often comes up often when living in control.** I would expect her to read my mind about what to do or prioritize next. It was a recipe for disaster. If life went sideways, which it did when I was trying to control it all, and she didn't do exactly the things that I wanted her to do, I would get frustrated.

There was a point where we were both highly irritated with each other to the point that it was affecting our work (and my income). I took a long, honest look at myself as an employer and said, "Is this really her fault? Am I setting her up for success?" As long as I was controlling everything, I wasn't really setting her up for success. I decided, "If this isn't about me and the need to control, if I am giving her everything that she needs to be successful and she's not successful, then it's her. It's not me."

I also realized that if it didn't work out with her, if it wasn't about me controlling the situation, that I needed to have a success plan for my next assistant. I got really intentional with how I was communicating, how I was mapping out her tasks, and how I was documenting the processes she did daily – all of which I would need to help the next person be successful if she wasn't.

And guess what happened? She started being much more productive. I started trusting more in the process and in her because I was giving her the tools she needed, and she was creating the results with them. I had empowered her to do the things I required, and she felt empowered!

When I set her up with all the tools to do that, she began to enjoy her work more, and she got clarity on her purpose, deciding to go to work for herself as a coach. By the time she left, we were in a great place and I was excited for her to begin a new chapter where she felt prepared to overcome many of the fears she'd had in the past. And I had a better idea of what I needed to give someone to help them be successful.

I realized that in the beginning, when I was in control, I was setting us both up to fail. It was so incredibly frustrating. It was a waste of time. It was a waste of money. Through the process of being intentional and by giving up that control, when my next assistant started, it was much more automated. We were both able to get so much more done in a much more relaxed state of being, and there was so much less frustration and so much more joy.

And I see so many people doing that in business relationships and personal relationships. Not only does it waste time, money and emotion, but it perpetuates the cycle that only I can do it!

I had a similar experience when I hired my nanny. The first year of my son's life, I thought I was going to be the woman who did it all. I would try to work full time while being a full-time mom. And I did okay for the first six months until my son got mobile, and then it became a daily exercise of beating my head against the wall saying, "I'm failing at everything."

In a moment of vulnerability and frustration, I told my husband, "I need help." I needed help because I was failing at two things that are both incredibly important to me. I was failing at being present for my son, the entire reason that I created my own business. And I was failing in my business that I love, one where I have massive ability to impact others.

And when I said, "I need help," I took the first step to giving up control. I found someone who is still with me three years later. Why hadn't I done this earlier? Because I had guilt, thinking I was a fraud. Here I was, teaching women how to create an additional income stream or replace their income if they want to be home with their children, or just have more choices in their lives.

I was afraid I'd be a fraud if I admitted I couldn't do it all and hired help. The reality is, I'd created this incredible business and income that allowed me to be able to leverage my time. It allowed me to be able to get help!

On my nanny's first day, I realized I needed to leave the house, or I'd micromanage the whole process. I'd have to be in control. I wouldn't really let her do what I hired her to do, which is help me.

So I went and did a yoga class, and it was *exactly* what I needed. I hadn't been getting to the gym because I was too busy being busy, too busy controlling the situation, arguing for my excuses and proving myself right in keeping them.

The second day she was there, I went and got my nails done, something I'd wanted to do for weeks but hadn't made happen due to my excuses for not having someone watch my son. And I got a quick lesson in leverage, on why you hire people to help you do the things that need to be done so that you can do the things you really want to do.

That doesn't mean you're going to always be in a state where you're only doing the things you want to do, but the end result? I realized I could give up the control of being the one to do the laundry or grocery shopping.

I could give up control of tasks that weren't really crucial to me being relaxed, abundant and joyous.

And my birth experience was probably the most obvious example of this. When I was planning for my first birth, I did everything possible to prepare. I took two birthing classes in person. I took an online birthing class. I watched so many YouTube videos, crying every time the baby was born (partly for the joy, partly for the relief it was over)! I read books.

I was obsessed with what my birth experience was going to be like. The reality was that I had a ton of fear about not knowing how it was going to go down. I had so much fear, so I tried to control the process. My body, which needed to be relaxed, was beyond tense. I was afraid. I was doing the opposite of what I needed to have the experience I desired.

In nature, when an animal is giving birth, the baby could be halfway out, but if that animal feels threatened, they go into massive protection mode and can actually pull the unborn baby back in. Think about that. When you're experiencing fear and not trusting the process, you are causing your body to fight against the natural birth process.

As a result, I ended up with medication, something I didn't want. And while I had a healthy son and I was able to have the people there that I loved, I had regrets because I knew I hadn't released the things necessary to have the experience I envisioned.

Now, we can't plan out every detail of birth, though that hadn't stopped me from trying! I had an incredibly specific birth plan. On it, if I decided to ask for drugs, my "safe" word wasn't a word, it was the phrase "I care more about my own comfort than about the health of my child." Seriously?! I look back now and shake my head. I was being so judgmental of myself, so controlling. And of course what happened? That which I feared – that I ended up medicated.

With my second birth experience, I went into it with the fear released. I knew more of what to expect but I had a team there that I absolutely trusted. That's part of it, giving up the control by allowing others to help.

I also understood that being intentional meant trusting I'd have a healthy baby girl but that I didn't need to control every single moment. I prepared essential oils that were specific to certain parts of labor like nausea or pain, but I didn't think I *must* use every single one of these. I focused more on enjoying the process of preparing them and being intentional than focusing on at what moment they might be needed.

I took that philosophy to everything around my birth. It was an instrumental part of my being relaxed and that I had a quick, beautiful and natural birth. It was an incredibly intentional birth experience, and I am so grateful for it. It just showed me what can happen when we give up control and the beauty that can come from it.

There are so many different ways you can be intentional and numerous ways to give up control and just BE.

◆

TOOLS FOR *BEING*, #6
LET'S LET GO

Letting go isn't just about releasing old stories, emotions, or expectations. It's also about letting go of things in our lives that don't allow us to be in our BE state!

1. Write a list of all the things that you do, both in your personal life and in business. For example, "I do the dishes. I do the laundry. I hand-write client thank you cards." It can be things you do that you feel like you have to do, or that you feel like you're the only one that does them right.

_____

_____

_____

_____

2. Write a list of the things you'd *rather* be doing. These could be activities like TAKE A BATH!!! Sleep! Work Out! Take a dance class. Play games with your children!

_____

_____

_____

_____

3. On the first list, circle the things that someone else could be doing *or* that you could *stop* doing. What do you not like doing?

   What can you automate, delete, or delegate from List One? What will that open up time for?

Tasks to Automate: How:

_____

_____

_____

_____

Tasks to Delegate: To Whom:

_____

_____

_____

_____

Tasks to Delete: How:

_____

_____

_____

_____

You can also *swap!* Perhaps there's something you *really* enjoy doing or are great at that someone in your household or social circle detests. What possibilities are there for swapping out that chore or task with another person?

Personally, I don't like breaking down the recycling. I'll order and unpack groceries while listening to a podcast, and my husband does the recycling, enjoying the time outside! Swapping for the win!

4. On the second list, which of those things that you'd rather be doing, would you do first with more time? Pick one and commit to it! Whether you're someone that is more driven moving away from pain (the tasks you don't want to do) or toward pleasure (doing the fun things you are now incorporating), it's time to put ADD into practice and infuse more things that bring you happiness and joy into your life!

_____

_____

_____

_____

◆

This is not about doing more. It's not even about giving up some things to take on other things, even though if you enjoy those other things more, you're going to definitely be more in the BE state. They could be just the things that are going to help you BE more.

Last, don't go through the motions. You've got to really release that control. You've got to create a plan for it. Don't control the plan, just create a plan, but most importantly, create an intention around it.

Every morning, I have a daily clarity sheet that starts with my intention of how I want to be today. What is my ideal BE state? And there's typically one or two I will write down. And then what is my mantra or affirmation for today? It's not what am I going to control today.

When I start with that intention, it just creates so much clarity around where I'm going to spend my time and my energy and what I'll be doing, but it all starts with *being*. So go out there, be intentional, and release the control.

NON-NEGOTIABLES FOR BEING YOU

If you're like me, you might be a checklist or a to-do list girl. I can't remember a time in my adult life that I didn't have checklists for my day. I was constantly working to optimize my life, to get more organized, and to do more in my time. I equated productivity, or worse, busy-ness, with my value.

There were days that I was really productive and I checked off a ton of things, but it didn't feel like enough. I would look back and ask myself why I didn't feel better if I'd done so much. I had these crazy checklists that were 40 items long, and even if I accomplished 80% of it, I'd feel like I hadn't done enough. Busy does not equal good.

Other times, I would be vacationing or working remotely, and I'd wonder why I felt so good when I was doing less but often accomplishing more? Because I was doing things I felt called to do.

I had a realization this past year when my mentor, Cayla Craft, told me that balance is bullshit. I initially disagreed, thinking, "No, we can have balance. We just have to be organized. We just have to manage our time. It's possible."

Then I realized that was the perfectionist, the voice of control, talking. The reality is whether you're a mom, a business owner, or an employee, we're always juggling multiple things. And the idea that it's all going to fit into these perfectly little segmented pie pieces that are color coordinated is idealistic. When I started to embrace that balance wasn't really sustainable and started looking at non-negotiables, everything shifted.

First, designing your life is not about vacationing 24/7, it's not about not working, it's not about being irresponsible. In a day with nothing scheduled, how would you be? What would make you feel that way? It's about ensuring that you have the components that are important for you to live in your BE state.

Part of living a lifestyle of *being* relaxed, abundant and joyous is having the ability to travel, the ability to design my day – the ability to do what I wanted, with whom I wanted when I wanted, and where I wanted.

I thought back to early 2016 when I worked remotely while traveling with my husband. I had just replaced my corporate income with my network marketing side hustle. However, I wasn't leaving my job for income, as I had a great salary, I was leaving my job for lifestyle and freedom of choice. I was leaving my job so that when my husband was able to go to London or Milan or Sydney for work, I could go with him.

That winter, he had two conferences that were in Australia over a two-week period. I just had to pay for my flight to join him, as his hotel and company dinners took care of the rest! I would get up at 6:00 a.m. Australian time, work out, then work from 7:30 to noon.

Afterward, I would meet a friend for lunch who was consulting remotely and also traveling with her husband, who worked with mine. We'd meet for lunch, go sightseeing or wine tasting. I'd come back and do an hour of e-mails before meeting my husband for dinner and a show or activity. It was the best 12 days.

I looked back at that time and asked myself why that trip was so wonderful. I was still getting a lot accomplished. I wasn't checked out completely. My business was flourishing even though I was only putting in four to five hours a day of work. And I realized it was because I was really clear on my priorities and I was doing the things that I wanted to do, but also was doing non-negotiables for really enjoying myself.

Let's break down your non-negotiables, starting with your day. Think about this as a recipe for *being*. You have those qualities that you want to live in, but what are the ingredients that help you to achieve it?

Number one, for me, is sleep. I function well on seven hours of sleep if it's *good* quality sleep. But if I don't sleep well, long enough, or during the optimal hours, I don't feel my best self. I'm not creative. I'm not as patient with my child. I find myself busy and overwhelmed without really being productive. And because I can't live in my BE state while exhausted, sleep is one of my non-negotiables.

Number two is nourishment, fueling my body so I can feel my best and do my best. Ensuring I'm well hydrated, that I'm getting in one or two plant-based protein smoothies, whole foods like veggies and nuts, and healthy fats like avocado. By hydrating and properly nourishing my body, I'm ensuring I don't deal with low blood sugar or dehydration, which both kill your mental abilities and creativity. It doesn't mean that I eat perfectly or obsessively, but it means I ensure I'm counting my nutrition, not my calories.

Next is movement, which looks different for everyone. It doesn't mean you have to wake up in the morning and do an hour at Soul Cycle, even though that's a phenomenal way to start your day. Some days it's just as simple as walking outside or doing 10 minutes of body weight exercises that make me sweat. It's about moving my body.

Number four on my list is quiet. Although I consider myself an extrovert, I realized I need to refill and charge my batteries. That can look like meditation or a few minutes outside in nature or a massage. Taking that time to just reset myself to stop the noise and flurry of things around me and give myself a chance to be quiet, to meditate, and to listen.

Next is connection, beginning with my family first. While I work from home and spend lots of time with my kids, it is also about quality connection. It really means getting down on my kids' level, not just being near them on my laptop. My son is almost four years old and loves to play! That means doing a dance party in the morning or having "mommy time" playing outside or having connection time that's just about him, without any other distractions. It equals play and joy!

 If you have young children (or a dog), there's no better example of being than them in their natural state! Spend time with them doing what they want! Abandon the agenda!

With my daughter, as a baby, it's usually lying on my bed, cuddling, smiling, and listening to a meditation or talking quietly to her while she babbles back. Just breathing in her smell, making her feel safe and loved. It doesn't mean we have to be doing an exercise to further her child development, for the best development is built on the foundation of *being* present with her.

Connection also means nurturing my relationships with friends and clients. Ideally, these connections happen in person where I have the chance to actually hug someone, but sometimes it is a connection that happens online. I prefer voice memo to text, phone to voice memo, zoom to phone and in person to anything else! It's not the time you spend, it's how you spend the time.

Finally, gratitude is also crucial and part of my daily routine. If I'm feeling a little funky or moody, it's usually due to skipping my morning gratitude routines. I know to stop and write down (or say aloud) 10 things I'm grateful for. I often say them while showering each morning, starting by being grateful for the hot water, the soap, my ability to design my day, to do work that I love and to work from home.

And when I'm driving with my son, I ask him to talk about what makes today great. It's very simple, so a three-year-old can understand it, but it might be, "I am grateful for the blue sky today. I am grateful that we are driving in our car. I am grateful we have gas."

Understand, it is nearly impossible to feel anxious and practice gratitude. Don't believe me? Try it!

Whenever I feel anxious or stressed, my first go-to is to think about what I am grateful for in this moment. What am I learning? Because it totally will flip the mood. And a great day is one that anxiety does not take control.

To sum up, my non-negotiables for my day, in no particular order: sleep, nourishment, movement, quiet, connection, and gratitude.

That's a simple list, but when I get them in, it's a recipe for a wonderful day. When I do, I go to bed feeling so much better about my day and so excited for the next. It's not about the hours you put in a day, it's about what you put into those hours!

Now, for extra credit, a few bonuses for an exceptionally abundant day!

JOY! Every day I try to do something that is joyous. A lot of times I get that naturally from my connection time with my son. That can be just being really present with whatever I'm doing, or it can be doing something I'm passionate about. If I take a ballroom dance class or doing something creative or focus on giving to someone else, I am going to be in a state of joy.

And joy is nearly always a result of ensuring my first non-negotiables.

Growth is another fantastic ingredient. Without growth, we become stagnant. You want to be constantly growing. Growth could be a podcast or a book or course or something that is putting information and inspiration into my mind. And that inspires me to be even more inspired and to be more creative.

The final ingredient is something I call "loving on." You could also call it a random act of kindness or giving. It can be sending a couple of texts or a voice memo to someone you love. Sending a "thinking of you" card. Donating to a charity someone you care about loves. Buying groceries for the person behind you in line. It's loving or giving back with no expectations.

My question for you is, what are your non-negotiables for your day.? Make a list of 10 or 15 of them and then get clear on what is the most important!

◆

TOOLS FOR *BEING*, #7
YOUR NON-NEGOTIABLES
FOR BEING YOU

Start with a list of things you'd love to have in your day! Think back to a great day you've had and reverse engineer the activities you did, the building blocks that were part of a day you went to bed being grateful for.

Examples: meditation, time outside, movement, nourishing your body, prayer, listening to something positive, dancing, great sleep, affection, finishing something, family time, catching up with a friend, cooking. List as many as possible!

_____

_____

_____

_____

Next, what is *really* important? What are the things you want to do and experience to feel at your best, day after day? Are there those that will *absolutely* help you feel your best self? Your most connected? Your most giving? Pick 3-5.

_____

_____

_____

_____

Let's extend that out for the week. What are your non-negotiables for the week? You don't need to wait until Mondays to start. You can begin any time of the week. Is it a date night? An afternoon with your child at the park? Taking a class to learn more about something you love? A mani/pedi?

Weekly:

Examples: Date night, family time, giving back, taking a class, self-care.

_____

_____

_____

After that, you can think about the month. What do you need every month to feel phenomenal, to love your life?

Monthly:

Examples: Date night, family time, giving back, taking a class, self-care.

_____

_____

_____

◆

Next, plan it in!! Things don't happen unless we make time for them. And if they are a priority, we must make the time! Remember, do anything you can to be happy, because when you are happy, you can do anything!

Before I plan out the next month, I like to do a review of the month past, to see what worked, what didn't and what could be improved. It's about constantly evolving!

Finally, let's talk about your year. We overestimate what we can get done in a day, but we really underestimate what we can get done in the year. Part of designing your year is taking a review of the year before. At the end of the year, you can look back at the goals you set last year and assess how you did.

Have an honest sit-down session with yourself and see how you feel about what you accomplished. Reviewing your year helps you design the next year and be intentional about creating a foundation. And if the tools and materials you used for the past year weren't the best ones, level them up. That's the beauty of you designing your life! You can make the changes.

TOOLS FOR *BEING*, #8
PLAN A DAY FOR YOURSELF

Plan a day with yourself (or your significant other or friend) to plan out the year ahead. What's important to you in your month, weeks, and days? Do you have any creative projects you'd love to do? Do you finally want to learn that foreign language and then take the trip you've been talking about for a decade? Look at what worked or didn't last year and find ways to optimize it.

☐ Check it Off!

☐ Date Scheduled _____   ☐ Time Scheduled _____

☐ Location _____

☐ Completed _____

Gift: Visit www.becomingyou.co/designtime for a template of planning your yearly Life Design session!

THE BE VS. DO STRUGGLE

Every June for the past few years, we have done a family trip with our best friends. Three years ago, we went to Spain when Luca was just a few months old. Last year it was France, and this year, Hawaii.

The day we arrived, I was sitting at the pool and felt a debilitating wave of anxiety. Why? I was scrolling Instagram stories and I suddenly felt a need to be posting. Then I looked up at the vibrantly blue skies, inhaled that magical Hawaiian smell of flowers and sea, and listened to the sound of the water splashing and my child laughing. I took a deep breath and grounded myself. I reminded myself, "Be here now."

One of my dear friends, a speaker, business coach, and mom of three, Kari Keating, says, "Be where your feet are." She was discussing the struggle that moms experience with splitting time between building a business and parenting. It's something so many of us struggle with, whether it's our kids and our business, or our significant other and friends, or working and relaxing.

The reason I constantly talk about our BE state, the state of being that we want to be in, is because I haven't mastered it. Not every day. I'm aware that focusing on it, practicing it, and working on it gives me the tools and the awareness to overcome a lot of the anxiety and the challenges I've had in my past. But it's an ongoing practice. It's a muscle I have to keep training or it grows weak.

And let's be real! Hawaii is a really easy place to BE. There's an unrushed vibe. The locals are smiling. The weather is perfect! There's a reason that on vacation when we enjoy ourselves, we daydream about leaving our normal life and staying in that vacation spot forever. We talk about quitting our jobs and bartending or opening up a tiny little boutique or a juice bar. But it's not about you living in this vacation state that makes us yearn for vacation. It's that you spent your days BE-ing. Our purpose is to find out how to BE more of the time so that we build a life we don't need a vacation from.

When I met my husband, I was the queen of productivity, the queen of the do. In the beginning of our relationship, before we were married, every time we'd take a road trip or we'd be on a long drive, I'd want to listen to an audio book together or a book of questions. On a long drive from L.A. to Vegas the first year we dated, I literally brought a book called 4,000 Questions for Getting to Know Anyone and Everyone. I probably made it through interviewing him on 40 of those questions before he was like, "Let's have some quiet time."

A little further into the relationship, I started to use that time to edit photos or take a phone call for my side hustle or answer e-mails. I just loved that I could get things done while he was basically chauffeuring me. He didn't love it because he felt like a chauffeur! Over time, it became a thing that frustrated him. He'd say, "Let's just share some windshield time," which drove me crazy because I couldn't make progress or order groceries or read.

But what does windshield time really mean? It's time to energetically sync up, to share space, to share air. As parents, where we don't have as much quiet time together, that's our time to hold hands or just to enjoy the landscape or listen to music or a podcast. It means that every minute doesn't have to be spent planning, because when we're planning, we're focusing on the future, not in the now.

Believe me, I am a lover of list-making, and on my to-do list, I actually list redo my calendar, plan out my week, redo my goal list. That's dessert to me. I look forward to it. It's the "designing a life" part that I'm all about.

But when are you taking the time to love that life you're designing? Are you so busy building a life that you aren't taking time to actually live it? Let me repeat that.

Are you so busy building that life that you aren't taking time to live it?

What's causing most of your anxiety? Typically it's focusing on something outside of what we're experiencing now, on a future time, on a different place, on something else we could or should be doing, on someone else other than ourselves.

The first morning we woke up in Hawaii, I asked my husband how he was feeling. "Relaxed," he said. I asked him if he'd already meditated. He said, "No, I deleted Gmail off my phone for the trip."

So simple, yet so powerful. He recognized the source of his anxiety and neutralized it. How can we recognize the things that take us out of our BE state, that trigger distraction or anxiety, that ultimately keep us from living our best life, that keep us from being our best selves?

A few years ago I was on a trip with a friend. We were sitting in this incredible restaurant in a city most people just dream of visiting. We had ordered champagne to celebrate life, and right after we toasted, she dove into her phone to post on social media and to engage with her followers. I remember feeling sad as the champagne grew warm because she was focusing energy on creating an experience for her followers to see instead of BE-ing in that experience with me.

Often what triggers us most in others is actually something within ourselves we are meant to work on. How often have I done this? When I make my husband retake a photo because it isn't flattering, or I miss my child's smile because I was absorbed in a book about being a better parent, or focusing all my energy in planning a romantic evening out instead of just getting lost in the romance of a simple cuddle with my husband on the couch.

Be here now. Being in the moment is a little island that anxiety rarely visits. There is a reason they call it the present, and we need to use that gift.

GOING OFF THE GRID - DISCONNECT TO CONNECT

Do you pride yourself on being a multi-tasker, yet you never quite feel like you can take a breath? Or if you just pull one more all-nighter or late night, you'll be all caught up and be able to enjoy that weekend ahead? The reality is that we never get caught up if we prioritize everyone and everything before ourselves.

Have you ever gone anywhere and realized you had no cell phone reception? Or forgot your charger and after that initial panic wore off, you realized the day seemed somehow more vibrant? You found it easier to breathe, or that you had more meaningful conversations?

That's exactly how I felt easing back into work life after eight weeks of maternity leave. The first few weeks after my daughter was born, I did nothing except what I wanted to. A lot of self-care, a lot of napping. I barely looked at my phone. I didn't open my computer for more than a week. And it felt delicious. And I realized I didn't miss much of what I wasn't doing.

Being present for the time after having a baby is something most people recognize as important and hopefully prioritize. But how quickly we can fall back on the routine of those busy, connected lives.

A few weeks after returning from maternity leave, I had a little kick in the butt reminder when I e-mailed my coach and received her out of office response. "Thank you for your recent note. I will be disconnecting and on vacation from Wednesday, May 29th to Monday, June 3rd. If you hear from me during this time, tell me to knock it off and rest harder. I look forward to getting back to you when I return." I thought, "Yes, way to go! Way to actually disconnect on vacation and enjoy yourself."

When my first child was born, I loved the time spent bonding while he nursed. The first couple days it was the most wonderful thing, feeling connected, feeling present. Time just unfolded beautifully. When I went back into work life, I purchased all of the things on Amazon that promised to help me be more productive, like the laptop buddy that lets you have a baby on your lap while working.

One day I looked down and he had fallen asleep. He wasn't even nursing anymore, and I hadn't even noticed. I was so engaged in what I was doing that I was not being present for this beautiful moment that was only going to be for a small part of my life. I felt really disconnected and sad. I set an intention that I wouldn't nurse while at my computer. Instead, I would go into my bedroom and meditate or nap with my baby or just gaze at him.

I used some of this non-working quiet time to read a book called **The Hands-Free Momma** by Rachel Mary Stafford. If you are a parent, you deserve to read this book. It provides principles on how to be more intentional with your kiddos. When I utilize them, my life is so much richer and I feel like a calmer, happier parent and human.

Three tips from the book that encompass *being*:

1.   Put what is important in front of what is urgent.

What looks urgent is the pile of dishes, the unfolded pile of laundry, and the million e-mails that never go away. They all look urgent because there are things and people clamoring for your attention. The things that are important are your child that would love to be playing with you. It is your spouse who would love it if you just walked over and gave them a hug, sat on their lap, kissed them, or just told them how much you appreciate them.

Our work will *always* seem urgent. Our desire to empty the notifications on our phone or get our e-mails under control. My toddler taught me this lesson when he started saying, "Mom, look at me. Mom, look at me." One day he said, "Mom, look me in the eye." That was an "a-ha" moment for me. He said that was because I was looking at my phone or my laptop. He was asking for my attention and nothing is more important than him. What's important may not advocate for itself as loudly as urgent does, so it's up to you to advocate for important!

TOOLS FOR *BEING*, #9
WHAT'S IMPORTANT TO YOU?

What's Important to You?

_____

_____

_____

What's Urgent?

_____

_____

_____

How can you better prioritize important over urgent?

_____

1. **Build a habit of peace and renewal instead of getting something accomplished.**

That can be meditation or taking a midday walk. I know when I started meditating, I questioned whether it was really important. Wouldn't that 10-15 minutes of not doing anything be better used to get something done? That question showed that I wasn't prioritizing BE-ing. What I have learned through my practice of meditation is that when I don't invest that 10 or 15 minutes in my state of BE-ing by meditating, I get less done but feel busier.

What creates peace within you? How can you renew yourself throughout the day?

_____

_____

_____

2. **PLAY!** In Hands-Free Mama, she emphasizes the importance of a parent telling a child, "I love watching you play." Children always play, and it's important to take time to notice them.

   I taught Luca to say, "Play is my *job!*"

   And why isn't it ours? How often are you playing? Are you even experiencing play? What's the point of going 24/7 if we're not enjoying ourselves or if we're missing those moments, those opportunities to play and be present? It's not enough for you to simply watch your children play. It's important that you get out and play as well.

How can you play? Where can you fit in 10-15 minutes a few times throughout the day? Notice how joy emerges!

_____

_____

_____

 TIP Keep a menu of different play activities on your phone so you have several to choose from! Now, go set an alarm to remind yourself to play a few times throughout the day!

This message is not just for moms, though. Anywhere you go, you see people on their phones. Or working long hours without a break. You see people out to dinner, and they're both glued to their phones. Be present with the person you're with. My husband taught me that lesson as well.

When I first started building my side hustle business to leave my full-time job, I was working like crazy. I understood the power of compression and doing it quickly, and it absolutely paid off. The time I invested gave me the freedom that I now have, but it came at a cost.

My husband would get home from work and I would be entirely plugged into a phone call or to the computer, and he'd get so irritated. I would justify my actions because I was doing this to create more choice in *both* our futures, but it didn't change the fact that he didn't feel important.

He wanted to feel connected when he got home and all it took was a simple greeting and 10 minutes to chat with him about his day. Once I understood that, I'd ensure I was off the phone to give him a few minutes of quality time so he felt appreciated and connected, and then I'd be back to building our dreams.

◆

TOOLS FOR *BEING*, #10
CHECK IN

When are the times you find yourself feeling frustrated, over-whelmed, or less than?

_____

_____

When are you multitasking without joy or going through the motions?

_____

_____

When do you feel like you're letting down the people who you love?

_____

_____

◆

There's no reward to be won for depriving yourself of the very thing you are working hard for.

As you read this, you are probably saying, "Yes, yes, but I'm an entrepreneur. I'm a business owner. I need to be plugged in. Everyone is relying on me. It's expected." The question is, what is being plugged in costing you?

When you lay down at night, are you thinking about memory points of what happened throughout the day, those magic moments? Or are you getting sleepy staring at the blue light of your phone, scrolling on Instagram, or returning e-mails?

It's a slippery slope, because it can start with one thing – I'm just going to check my phone once at dinner. Or I'm going to just take my phone to bed for five minutes. And suddenly you're plugged in 24/7. If you are building another business or you are building a second stream of income in order to give you more time, there are still ways you can set boundaries to feel so much more present in your life and so much less pulled.

Here are five rules that I developed for myself. I'm human, so I am not 100% perfect about using them. And when I'm not, I get the wake-up call that I missed that moment with my child or that my husband is frustrated and disconnected with me, and it reminds me to recommit to them and myself.

1. Complete your morning routine before checking your phone. Your morning routine could include meditation, exercise, affirmations, or all of them! Go back to your list of non-negotiables or read Hal Elrod's book **Miracle Morning**.

2. Set times that you'll check your social media. Put it in your calendar! I pull up social media when I need to pee! Seriously! It allowed me to like a few things, comment, or save an inspirational post for later. Doing it then kept me from pulling my phone out when I was on the computer doing work or from the distraction of checking my phone when I'm with my child.

 Put It in Your Calendar!

The biggest culprit and time distraction from our goals can come from social media. We all know how easy it is to check Instagram and fall down the scroll hole! Suddenly, 10-15 minutes pass as we allow somebody else's filtered life to stop us from living ours. If you aren't required to post on social media for your business, delete it from your phone. There are also some great apps like Planoly or Later that you can create your content and have them pre-posted.

Another idea is to use a tracking app to see your usage. There's one called Moment on the iPhone. Just being cognizant of what we're doing can help us change our habits.

One tip that works for me more than anything is to turn off notifications on your social media. It's a game changer. I went in and turned off all of the notifications in my phone except for my text messages. I let people know if it's an emergency or urgent, don't e-mail me, don't Facebook message me, don't Instagram message me, just send me a text. This allows you to be intentional about going in and interacting with your e-mail or your social media. It also reminds you that social media is *never* urgent or an emergency.

3. Set times to check and respond to e-mails. You need to train people on what to expect because there is no award for returning e-mails at 3:00 a.m. If somebody is saying, "Wow, you're incredible because you return e-mails at 3:00 a.m.," are they valuing the same things that you are?

Set up an out-of-office message. I used it while I was on maternity leave, and I find it helpful when other people use it, too. It makes me feel good that they are setting boundaries, and it shows me that they value themselves. When we are up front and notify people of what to expect, it shows people that we value ourselves as well.

You can also create a note on your e-mail signature that says I return e-mails from 12:00 to 1:00 and 4:00 to 5:00. Set the rules for yourself, and then train people to follow them.

4. Create phone rules or boundaries. For us, at 4:00 p.m. during my "happy hour" where I play with my son for an hour, the phone is out of sight. It stays there through dinnertime and bedtime. I'll glance at it once an hour before my husband gets home to see if he's updated me on his schedule, but I don't respond to other text messages unless they are urgent.

If I go back to work after my little ones go down to sleep, I'll do it from my computer instead of from my phone. When I sit down at my desk, I'm less likely to get distracted, and I even return text messages on iMessage. It's faster because I have the whole keyboard and I don't get distracted by social media because I don't open up the browser for Facebook or Instagram!

5. Leave the phone out of the bedroom, and if you use your phone as an alarm, keep it away from your bed. You'll be less likely to grab it if you have trouble falling asleep. And guess what? You'll probably have less trouble falling asleep if you create some great hygiene around phone usage.

Don't pull the phone out if you're on a date night or while spending time with your significant other.

To have intimacy, you need to do things together. If you watch TV, put the phones down and cuddle together.

I was chatting with a friend and she was telling me that she and her significant other aren't intimate very often. As we talked about it, we realized that it came down to the fact that at night they were sitting there watching TV, and they're both on their phones. Phones are much less of an aphrodisiac than a good snuggle session or massage!

When you're with other people, put down the phone, because no one on social media is more important than the person in front of you. If you feel like someone on social media is, maybe you need to re-evaluate the time you're spending with whomever you're with.

Re-read through the list of five. Which one you can incorporate today? Just *one* will create so much more space and ability to breathe in your life. Then find someone who can hold you accountable. My husband and I hold each other accountable!

Most importantly, check in with how you feel as you make these changes!

TOOLS FOR *BEING*, # 11
PHONE CHALLENGE

For the next couple of days, go somewhere and leave your phone at home. If you have kids or you need to be reached in case of an emergency, just tell them where you're going. They can call a landline or who you're with if it's an emergency.

And understand that just like detoxing from sugar, caffeine, or anything out there designed to be addictive, you're going to feel a little panicked initially! But then you are going to feel so, so good!

☐ Completed Phone Challenge!

CHAPTER 6

Happiness Is A Choice I Make

"Happiness comes from you."
— BEYONCE

BE-ing is the way, not the result. The more we BE, the more we are. Our world won't change unless we do. The more you BE, the more you'll be.

Being in action is not the same as BE-ing in action (BE + Action). BE-ING is the focus, not the action. Action without BE-ing will run you in circles.

Sometimes, when you are feeling off, a little action is a terrific fire starter. When you feel unmotivated to go to the gym, getting there and getting 10 minutes in changes everything!

But that action is driven by how you want to BE! Simply ask the question, "Would going to the gym help me feel and be healthier and more fit?" The answer will lead you to act.

WE DON'T NEED TO KEEP SEARCHING

Every Monday, I arrange fresh flowers throughout my house. They are usually purchased at Trader Joes or at the farmer's market. One morning,

I went to store things in our detached garage. It had been several days since I'd been out there, and I was pleasantly surprised by the beautiful roses blooming all over the sidewall of the garage! I cut some and brought them back into the house!

How often are we searching for knowledge, fulfillment, or fun from outside sources? Whether it be inspiration or clothing, we often forget what we already have in favor of that which is new and shiny.

Take a walk through your own resources, your natural talents, and your own strengths. What you already have there just needs to be acknowledged and allowed to shine!

What is your superpower? (Hint: it's typically something you take for granted but that amazes other people. Perhaps it's your ability to always find a kind thing to say, to whip up something delicious with anything in the fridge, to do mental math in your head, or to figure out the positive in any challenge.)

 What do people tell you, "Wow, that was so helpful" for?

Your Super Powers _____

_____

_____

Are you spending time using and cultivating them? Or are you yearning for different ones, letting your cape gather dust, unused?

Decide you are enough. Treat yourself as the subject of your own crush.

You are the most important person in your day, every day, because your relationship with yourself is the filter on every relationship and interaction that exists in your life. No matter where you go, you take yourself. How are you treating *you*?

Don't wait for your life to improve for you to improve. For you to feel better to start getting healthier. For that raise before you can change the situation that's draining you. For that other person to apologize first. To reach out to that person you admire.

You must be your own flashlight, finding your way with your vision before your feet get there.

If the right people aren't showing up in your life, change you first.

If the right opportunities aren't appearing, look a different direction.

If you don't like what you see, change your focus.

If there never seems to be enough, where can you find abundance?

When you become your biggest fan, not out of protection but out of real self-love, life shifts in a way that it will be happening *for* you, not *to* you. The journey to being your own ally, your own best friend, and your biggest supporter isn't easy, but it's not complicated.

TRUST YOUR INTUITION, YOUR COMPASS.

Shortly after my son was born, I had my first personal coaching session since I became a mama. I'm a huge believer in coaching to improve results in my business, health, and relationships because I do better with accountability and a kick in the rear end.

And since everything changes when a family of two become three, I invited my husband to be part of it to help hold me accountable.

I went in knowing it would get uncomfortable, because we were going to examine the results from our personal assessments. Nothing like an unbiased breakdown of your personality!

Staring your weaknesses in the eye isn't fun. Or getting raw about why we do what we do. The hour after the session I was emotionally drained, reflective, and a little defensive. But I was also more educated about myself and my role in the results I get in my life.

Working on yourself is very much like farming. You plant the seeds, water them and do the work long before results start to show. And you have to do it consistently or those seeds will dry up (like belief) or be overcome by weeds (distractions, fear). When you start to see the first buds, they are even more vulnerable to prey! So you continue to tend to them, take care of them and breathe life into them, just like we do those early results from any endeavor or change.

Weeding out negativity (distractions, naysayers) isn't something you do once. You must do it over and over and over.

The truth? The yield tastes so much sweeter when you've done the work yourself.

LIVING A LIFE OF BIG MAGIC WITH THE FOUR AGREEMENTS

The reality is, we don't operate in a bubble. We're always working to improve ourselves and design our lives in a world where we are constantly interacting with other people who have their own experiences, their own fears, their own dreams, and their own needs. Navigating our own boat against the constantly moving currents of others requires patience, humor, and tools!

There are two books that have been instrumental to me for staying true to myself and *being* while also doing my best in the way I interact with others. One is called **The Four Agreements** by Don Miguel Ruiz. The second one is **Big Magic** by Elizabeth Gilbert.

In **The Four Agreements**, Ruiz begins with the first agreement, to be impeccable with your word. That means speaking with integrity and saying only what you mean.

1. Be impeccable with your word.

Most people don't intentionally lie, or at least, don't set out to. I've realized with myself that I would often overcommit, because I didn't want to hurt someone's feelings by saying no. And that comes from a place of wanting to please. However, with overcommitting, it means I'm ultimately not pleasing myself or someone else, when I don't have the ability to BE and do to my fullest.

Another way to address integrity is looking at the excuse, "I don't have time." The reality is that we all have time. It's what we are choosing to focus our time on, or what we choose to do in our time, that determines how we spend it. Instead of making the excuse, be more careful with your words and say what you mean.

It's also about being honest with ourselves and others. I'll ask my husband, "Honey, would you like to take out the garbage? What I really mean is, "Could you please take out the garbage?" Speaking with integrity means being clearer on what you're asking for.

It is also important to not speak against yourself. This is a really powerful one, and it has to do with our self-talk. What do you say to yourself? In **Big Magic**, Gilbert says, "Argue for your limitations, and you get to keep them." How true is that? If someone tells us we should do something, and we give an excuse that we aren't capable of doing it, then we are arguing for that limitation.

In the same way, if someone tells us we can't do something and we say these are the reasons I will, then that is also true. How are we talking to ourselves? What if we talk to ourselves as if we were talking to the person we love the most? We should focus on self-love the most because when we don't love ourselves, everyone around us gets less than they deserve.

The next point in being impeccable with your word is avoid gossiping about others. Let's face it, this is a hard one. Often when we're hurt by someone, our first response is to either lash back out at them or to go to other people to be validated and get their support. But in that, we are devaluing the person who we were hurt by in order to minimize that hurt.

Have you ever felt better when you've done that? You call up a friend and complain about that person that hurt you, but do you ever feel better? Sometimes we feel better because we vented, but after that initial pressure release of emotion, when we're less worked up, we feel just as bad or worse.

We have a finite amount of time and energy in our lives, and if we use that time to complain about others, criticize others, or to find fault in others, that's time we are taking away from those people we love or are committed to serving. That is time that can be spent working toward our dreams or to give to those in need. It's time we will never get back.

If you're out there criticizing things that you don't support, why aren't you instead spending that time lifting up things that you are about? You have a limited amount of energy, and when it goes toward something that drains it, it's energy poorly spent, instead of energy invested (and expanded) toward something that recharges you and does good in the world.

And finally, in the practice of being immaculate or impeccable with our word, use your words in the direction of love and truth. What would your highest and best self say?

My husband and I were driving back one weekend from Carmel, California. I was tired and frustrated and definitely not being my highest and best self. He said something that I didn't like, and my first response was to snap back.

Instead, I asked myself, how would my highest and best self be, do, and say?

And instead of snapping back, I reached over, held his hand and I said, "Honey, I love you."

Now it can feel a bit phony at first, but doing that is not the same as faking it until you make it. It means that what you focus on expands. Where we put our energy, it grows. If we focus our energy on being kind and loving and honest, we will feel kind and loving and honest.

Even though I was still a little irritated, about 10 seconds later I started thinking about all the reasons I love my husband. Then I felt it. I felt lovingly toward him. I was no longer irritated. It is easier when we take away the emotion when we're worked up.

2. Don't take anything personally.

Number two from **The Four Agreements** is "Don't take things personally." That can be difficult as well. But the first part that Don Ruiz talks about is nothing that others do is because of you. And again, it can very much feel differently. I had a coach who once reminded me that in any conflict when the other person is snappy, before you snap back, ask yourself if they are hungry, tired, or stressed? About 95% of the time when someone is snappy with you or says something or does something to offend you, they are likely hungry, tired, or stressed. I know in our marriage, if my husband or I are not living in our BE state, it's almost always one of those things.

The other important part of asking that question is when you realize the people around you are hungry, tired, or stressed, it makes you realize it's not about you. But if you react to them in that state, it becomes about you and now there is a conflict.

So I ask that question and then silently ask to give them grace. I give them space, and most of the time, the other person will come back grateful. There's no emotion around it, and it shows the other person that you care about them, not about "winning" the situation.

Another thing to consider that what others say and do is a projection of their own reality and stories. When I started my network marketing business, I discovered that so many people had very strong opinions. I fell in love with a product line that I use, Isagenix, without even knowing it was network marketing.

But when I started looking seriously at network marketing, I realized I had this myth in my head around it. I met so many people that were either so gung-ho into it or the opposite and they hated network marketing. Whatever they felt about it, though, it was just a projection of their own reality.

When you're immune to the opinions and actions of others, you won't be a victim of needless suffering. For a moment, consider which is more painful – not doing what you are called to do and leading a life of regret because someone criticized you or judged you, or being wounded with a pinprick of someone's opinion that hurt for just a couple of weeks? It depends on how long you have dwelled on it, but to me, not bringing to life something you were uniquely meant to do is much more painful.

Over the course of your life, it will grow like a cancer. It will grow and the long-term pain it will give is so much greater.

In **Big Magic,** there were two things Elizabeth Gilbert said that speak to this. First, "Grieve if you must, but grieve efficiently." So when someone hurts you or you feel hurt by whatever they did that was based on their reality, grieve if you must, but grieve efficiently and quickly.

And lastly, "You do not need anyone's permission to live a creative life." What she means by a creative life is that you create a life where you set the terms and where you don't need anyone else's permission.

3. Don't make assumptions.

Find the courage to ask questions and express what you really want. I had to think, am I assuming that what this person said is about me? Because it might not be. There might've been something absolutely different that she just felt really worked up about that she was wanting to criticize someone or get her feelings out there. It may have not been about me at all. So don't make assumptions.

4. Always do your best.

Your best is going to change from moment to moment. You can measure your value by your dedication to your path, not by your successes and failures. I love that because so often I feel that we do measure our value from our successes or failures instead of by how hard we worked on it, by our dedication to bring to life whatever it is we are called to do.

And you know what is never our best? It's self-sabotaging because we're afraid, whether that's afraid of failure or fear of others' opinions. Elizabeth Gilbert, in **Big Magic,** says, "You do not get any special credit for knowing how to be afraid of the unknown." She explains how fear is boring because it always has the same result.

Last, do your best to avoid self judgement and regret. There are few things more painful than our own regret. You don't want regrets weighing on your when you breathe your last breath.

Elizabeth Gilbert said it beautifully, "Do you have the courage to bring forth the treasures that are hidden within you?"

READY. SET. GROW!!

I remember sitting down and reflecting the night before I launched my podcast. Less than a week before my daughter's due date. Reality – it was hard. Figuring it out, trying to not let perfectionism creep in. Messing up, re-recording, having to reschedule recording when this pregnant mama was too tired and sleep deprived to give what you all deserve to hear.

What's been harder? The growth. Questioning myself – about who I am to expect people to listen. Asking for help from others to make this a success (from my talented editor to the *incredible* human beings on the launch team). Not comparing myself to others (only using their examples for inspiration).

But you know what would be the hardest? Continuing to push down this calling from my soul to share not just my story and the things I've learned that I'm so grateful for, but the stories and insights of others that deserve a platform to shine.

It would be harder to know I could do this but letting learning something new, being vulnerable, having to ask for help, or being not so great at something while I'm learning *stop* me from evolving into who I am meant to be. It would be harder to wonder what impact could have been created – to ask "what if?"

Can I stay in bed all day? Well, technically yes, but I really can't stand being behind on my own dreams.

And total transparency, I don't always take my own advice. Often, what I teach is what I'm learning myself or what I require being reminded of.

I know that willpower is weakest in the evenings, so don't open that box of cookies (because one turns into five). And let's face it, even "healthy-ish and organic" isn't *that* healthy when you eat half the box.

And I know that I feel best when I go to bed early and get up early. Turning on the TV while I do stuff around the house and reorganize my desk is a *bad* idea because it never results in me feeling relaxed, abundant and joyous.

I paid for that late night the next morning. I was tired and cranky. Definitely not my best self when my toddler was using me as his personal jungle gym and I just wanted a minute of no one (or nothing) touching my body or needing something from me 24/7 (the pendulum of breast-feeding hormones swings the other way – from wanting to hug everyone to wanting to hug *no one*)!

How often do we do that? Do the things we want to do in the moment totally sabotage how we want to feel and be later? Instead of beating myself up all day about it, I chose to look at it as a reminder of *why* early-ish bedtimes have become my friend.

Sometimes, self-control equals self-love.

CHAPTER 7

Be More To Do More

*"The two most important days in your life are
the day you are born and the day you find out why."*
– MARK TWAIN

I used to pride myself on wielding my outlook calendar like a samurai sword. Appointments were opponents to be mastered and slayed. There was a sense of force in the *doing*. I needed to conquer the to-do list, overcome any challenges, and slay my goals.

Now, I'm working on wielding my BE qualities as Buddha beads – part of me, enhancing me, yet no need to call attention to them. There is no force in using them, only power.

FEAR + BEING (INSTEAD OF DOING) IT ANYWAY

Have you ever had a nightmare, asleep or awake, about public speaking? Where the thought alone inspired a cold, smelly sweat that drenched your clothes and a cortisol high? In high school Spanish, I used to get so nervous the first day before I had to introduce myself. I'd say it aloud over and over in my head and still criticize the way it came out.

Though I was pretty terrified of public speaking, I was also determined to do it. Maybe I was addicted to those fear hormones! However, it was nearly always in front of people I knew, so school plays or student council speeches, while still terrifying, were a way to get over my fears.

As an adult in my corporate job, I used to get so nervous before leading a team meeting. Even though I was training my employees or speaking to co-workers, I'd wait nervously for my turn, not even listening to those speaking before me because I was so wrapped up in my own head. I would try to memorize my content or have organized notes to not miss anything.

In 2014, I started working with an entrepreneurial coach to move past my fears. We didn't talk about speaking but about why I was so affected by what others thought, criticism, or conflict. I had many, many breakthroughs that shifted the attention I gave to others, the stories I created about situations or relationships and my own success, which allowed me much more time and energy to devote to those I wanted to.

In 2015, my coach pulled me up in front of an audience of strangers. I didn't realize that he had emotionally primed me for that moment. By not giving me time to stress, practice, or memorize, I was forced to ground into myself, to be in flow. I joke that it was the best speech or content I've ever done, but I barely remember what I said. I felt like I'd blacked out, but the reality is that I was letting my message and experience flow through me. Really, I had focused on *being*, not doing.

That day forever changed the way I've approached speaking. I used to seek it out to try to slay my fear dragon; now, I embrace it because I do want to share with others the lessons and strategies I've learned that may impact them. I don't get nervous, I don't sweat (much) and I don't obsess over every word.

Now, I have the privilege of speaking for my coach at his annual entrepreneur event, and I break down for the audience the Be vs. Do vs. Have states. The BE state allows for more creativity, more action, more joy, more love, and more impact. And being in it myself allowed me to experience all that.

START BEFORE YOU'RE READY

How many of you have a big dream or goal out there, but you're just not ready to take the next step? Or maybe it's even that first step. Maybe you bought a course but you feel like you need to take it before you create that e-mail capture you're working on, or you need to research the best course and talk to five other people that are doing what you're doing before committing to one. Or you're going to launch your business when you're ready, which means after you've done a never-ending list of things that have to happen first and you think you need figure it all out first.

Does that sound like you? My question is, when are you really going to be ready, and how do you get there?

I'd been thinking for a while about getting someone to do PR. One of the things I teach in my Brand Camp retreat is how to get yourself published. I've successfully submitted myself as an expert in productivity, branding, and healthy living to many publications, but I'm really ready to go to the next level.

I knew it was time to hire a PR person, but I'd been telling myself stories like, "Oh, I'm not niche enough. I'm not clear enough on what I'm talking about. I'm not ready. I need a product." Serendipitously, I chatted with a girlfriend of mine who had attended one of our Brand Camps and then decided to hire a PR professional, resulting in an incredible feature in the

New York Times. I finally decided, "You know what? Let's just schedule a fact-finding call. Do a little research."

What I found out is that I don't need to wait until I have released my book later or podcast or course or do the next *thing*. She could help me right now and bring incredible value. And that there are people out there looking for what I am currently doing. I don't need to accomplish the next three steps to be ready for PR.

It reminded me that people get stuck in what they don't know. I see it in social selling, network marketing, and entrepreneurship daily, excuses like, "I'll go to my first event once I'm making the money to pay for it."

I often ask them, "How do you think, without immersing yourself in something that's going to get you into action and get you clarity and belief, you're going to just figure it out and make that money? Unless you're willing to invest in yourself?" Even if you're not sure you're worth it, you are. And please, if you don't believe it yet, borrow my belief in you.

What is the problem? The problem is that you don't know what you don't know, and 90% of what we are afraid of is never going to happen. Typically, if you're not wasting 90% of your time worrying about the things that won't happen, you can actually dedicate that time to overcoming the things that will happen.

The solution is that action creates clarity. Action is the quickest way to learn. Life is a little bit like those Choose Your Own Adventure novels. Being a perfectionist and trying to figure out every possible outcome is like trying to go back whenever you don't like the choice you made. It's an absolute waste of time. In life and business, we can just go forward.

There is a feeling that we have when we are about to start something new. Leo Babauta wrote an article about it and called that emotion "joyfear."

It's the feeling that seems like anxiety, like your heart's racing or you've got a lump in your throat when you're about to do something you're not completely prepared for. I think it's like giving birth – you're so ready to be done with being pregnant, but when labor starts, joyfear is the perfect description for what you are feeling.

I want to give you five steps to start something before you are ready, because the idea of being ready is a total lie we tell ourselves.

TOOLS FOR *BEING*, #12
DREAM IT + BE IT

1. First, identify the next step toward your big goal or dream. Your next step to take that step so you can learn from that and grow from it and figure out what works. Then do your second one, and so on.

    What's your big goal or dream? What would you be so thrilled to look back 12 months from now and have accomplished or created?

    _____

    _____

    _____

    _____

---

2. Figure out your biggest excuse. What's the biggest excuse you're making that is stopping you from taking the next step? Chances are, it's "I'm not ready. I'm afraid. I don't want to make the wrong decision." But the reality is, most of the things we are afraid of actually don't risk death or bankruptcy. At worst, we're wasting time or energy, but we're wasting time now if we're not doing the thing that will move our business and our life forward.

What's your biggest excuse? _____

_____

What's the real fear behind it? _____

_____

3. How can you overcome that challenge? Reverse engineer the work. Break down those steps so it's a series of small moves instead of one big scary one.

   What are three micro-goals to accomplish it? Breaking goals into steps makes them less scary!

   a. _____

   _____

   b. _____

   _____

   c. _____

   _____

4. Next, commit to it. Tell someone you're going to take the step. This is one of the most valuable exercises. Make the commitment by telling someone when you are going to do it, someone who's going to hold you accountable. What is scarier than taking the next step? Telling someone you're going to take it and then not doing it.

Who are you going to tell your goal to? Don't just tell them *what* it is, tell them *why* you are committed to it! *How* will it change in your life or business? Who will it impact? How will you *feel*?

_____

_____

_____

_____

 Most people will get into more action moving *away* from pain than *toward* pleasure! Letting someone down by not getting into the action you committed to can be more motivating than the pleasure of achieving that goal!

TOOLS FOR *BEING*, #13
DOING THE WORK

Who are you telling? _____

_____

_____

What is the goal or action you are committing to? _____

_____

_____

_____

Why are you committed to it? _____

_____

_____

_____

How will it change your life or business? _____

_____

_____

_____

Who will it impact? _____

_____

_____

_____

How will you feel? _____

_____

_____

_____

How will you celebrate? _____

_____

_____

_____

☐ Check it off! When will you tell your accountability buddy? Set the date! _____

5. Last, get into action. Take a step toward it. You don't have to do it all, you just need to do something. Ask five people who are doing what you're doing well, what their top three tips are, and their top three challenges. What you're afraid of may not even be one of them.

TOOLS FOR *BEING*, #14
THE POWER OF FIVE

Write down the five successful people you will contact! What are their top three tips and top three challenges?

1. Person: _____

   Top Tips:

   1. _____

   2. _____

   3. _____

   Top Challenges:

   1. _____

   2. _____

   3. _____

2. Person: _____

   Top Tips:

   1. _____

   2. _____

   3. _____

Top Challenges:

1. _____

2. _____

3. _____

3. Person: _____

Top Tips:

1. _____

2. _____

3. _____

Top Challenges:

1. _____

2. _____

3. _____

4. Person: _____

Top Tips:

1. _____

2. _____

3. _____

Top Challenges:

1. _____

2. _____

3. _____

5. Person: _____

Top Tips:

1. _____

2. _____

3. _____

Top Challenges:

1. _____

2. _____

3. _____

Once you're in action, ride the momentum. There is no reason to slow down. If you took that one step, take another. If you spoke to the person about booking that event space for the workshop, do a poll between the two best dates. Reach out to possible speakers, form an interest list, but don't stop taking action because that is where the clarity comes from. And start before you are ready!

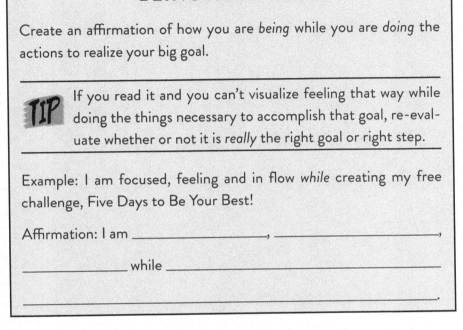

TOOLS FOR *BEING*, #15
BEING IN ACTION

Create an affirmation of how you are *being* while you are *doing* the actions to realize your big goal.

TIP If you read it and you can't visualize feeling that way while doing the things necessary to accomplish that goal, re-evaluate whether or not it is *really* the right goal or right step.

Example: I am focused, feeling and in flow *while* creating my free challenge, Five Days to Be Your Best!

Affirmation: I am _____, _____,

_____ while _____

_____.

Chapter 8

Well Being

*"We are not human beings having a spiritual experience.
We are spiritual beings having a human experience."*

– Pierre Teilhard de Chardin, French philosopher

Our body is our vehicle to have that human experience, to live our best life and to get us where we are meant to go. *Everyone* needs their health. Success and wealth mean little without our health. Our relationships and passions suffer when we don't have the energy to enjoy them. Even when we understand what our BE state is, it's nearly impossible to live in it if we are experiencing a sugar crash or digestive issues, if we are tired from lack of sleep or on edge with poorly managed stress.

Our health is *not* only dictated by what we put in our mouth. It's about understanding the relationship between our inputs into our body and what we get out. While a healthy mindset alone is one of our most valuable assets, it's supercharged when combined with a healthy, thriving body. Holistic health is about understanding the approach to applying the BE principles to our entire life, to finding the balance that creates real, sustainable change.

Understand that good health and a fit, energetic body are not a goal to hit, fall out of, then struggle back to. They can be a *state* we live in all of the time.

Because when we *feel* good, we do good!!

ASK YOURSELF:

How do you want to feel in your body?

What does *being* in my most abundant, relaxed, joyous body feel like? What does it require?

 How can I feel and BE with how I nourish, rest, and move my body?

How can I intentionally eat, move, and take care of my body for *being* my best self in order to create all the magic I'm meant to create?

How does my ideal self nourish herself?

Will this (food, exercise, decision) support me in feeling _____?

THE VALUE OF HEALTH

In December 2017, I attended Tony Robbins's Date with Destiny with my husband. We mapped out the current values system we've adopted through life and experience and then reprioritized them based on where we feel by asking "is _____ more vital than _____."

My old value system had Love & Connection at the top, but when I asked that particular question, another value kept going up the list until it stayed at the top. That value is Health. Even though I wrote it, I struggled a little with defining how health could be more important than love, especially given that I had spent the last four years in nearly perfect health but my times of most stress surrounded health challenges of those I loved the most.

A week later, as I spent my fifth day in bed with mono, pneumonia, and heartache after finding out I was going to miscarry, it was so clear. When you can't be present in your life because of physical challenges, it's nearly impossible to show or experience the love we are meant to feel.

Ten years ago, I watched my boyfriend lose his battle with Stage IV cancer. And though he was able to turn something horrific into something that inspired and moved many, we would all have traded in the inspiration and test of strength for his ability to live a long, beautiful life.

Twenty years ago, I watched my beloved grandmother's decline through Alzheimer's and Parkinson's. And even though she was physically there for a while, it was heartbreaking to not have her recognize the loving family she'd created.

Without health, it is nearly impossible to live our best life.

BE NOURISHED

There are nearly as many dietary theories and ideas as there are types of foods! With so many contrasting, polarizing opinions then food, and so many people touting their way as *the* way, it can be overwhelming to know what to try or whose advice to follow.

In all of my research and using myself as a guinea pig, the most sensible advice I've ever heard comes from Michael Pollan, New York Times best-selling author who has been writing about food and health for more than 30 years:

"**Eat** food. Not too much. Mostly **plants**."

Growing up on a farm, raising most of our food, and being the daughter of a fisherman who loved to hunt, I often ask myself, "Why eat like a king when you can eat like a farmer?"

The goal with food? To find the magic formula of eating for our greatest long-term health, for our daily fuel, and for our pleasure. To combine taste, tradition, and customs with convenience and sustainability. To not only look at what we eat and why, but when, as well as what we shouldn't eat and why.

Most importantly, check in with yourself, with your body, and ask yourself questions. Listen to your gut, literally, the source of your intuition.

ASK YOURSELF:

What does "eating for pleasure" mean to me?

Am I eating for the pleasure of the taste on my tongue or for the way I'll feel for the rest of the day after I eat it? Or both?

Will this (food, exercise, decision) support me in feeling _____?

YOU DON'T NEED A MONDAY TO CHANGE IT UP

"When you've got a kink in the creativity hose, you've got to circulate the energy around." — Peta Kelly

Last year, I felt *really* kinked. Some rough news about a friend's health triggered a lot of old anxiety for me and I was making less than superb choices by staying up too late, indulging in a glass (or two) of wine, and some senseless tv.

I wasn't feeling at all creative or inspired, but I also wasn't doing anything to change it. And while my to-do list could have fooled someone into thinking I was plodding along toward progress, my BE list wasn't fooling anyone.

After a few months of this, I decided to stop waiting for something to change how I felt and changed it myself – to invest into myself what I expected and wanted to get out. I cut out the "school night" wine, stowed the iPad, recommitted to exercise, ditched the late-night vegan cookies, and started going to bed earlier.

Within 24 hours, I felt like a different person, or rather, like the "old" me I was missing. The energetic, positive, bubbling, creative, fun, patient me. It's incredible how quickly things can change when we actually commit to *being* healthy, which makes doing the action easy, instead of just wishing for the change.

CHAPTER 9

Being Passionate And On Purpose

"No one has ever become poor by giving."

– ANNE FRANK

Do you ever feel you're on the path you're *supposed* to be on, yet your mind constantly wanders into what you're passionate about? Is passion something you save for your hobbies? Do you justify what you do for a living because it affords you the ability to live?

Why do we separate passion and purpose? It's possible to do well financially and to do massive good at the same time. I used to feel that I had to fit my passions into the pockets of my life, that you could either follow money or passion, but to possess both was a unicorn-esque rarity.

So I became a professional balancer, balancing 90-95% purpose (not the philanthropic kind, but the throw-myself-into-my-career-and-excel-at-all-costs kind) with 5-10% passion. It looked *really* good on paper and I convinced just about everyone I had it figured out. I just couldn't understand why I kept trying to convince my heart, because deep down, I was *not* buying it.

And six years ago, I was faced with that belief system. You see, my heart wanted a different reality. In my soul, I knew that you could have it all – the power to make an impact, an opportunity to have a career I was in love with, the ability to look forward to Monday mornings! It just took time for my ego and my need for security to listen that pull.

It's time to let that soul pull have a voice. Do something on the want list vs. the do list. Put your money where your heart is, not your mouth. Put your time where it's deserved, not needed.

When you mix passion and purpose together, you'll find yourself in your BE state so much more.

YOUR CALLING VS. YOUR LIVELIHOOD

Do you introducing yourself as what you do or who you are?

Is your identity come from your job or career? Or does it come who you are evolving into and what you are focusing on?

In my former corporate career, I knew that my title might impress people, but it didn't indicate who I was as a person. It didn't communicate my hopes, dreams, and interests. So I would answer, "I do this, but what I'm excited about is... "

Success defined by others didn't feel like I thought it would, and I was searching for my own happiness outside of empty milestones of goals met and achievements realized.

"Success that doesn't feel good isn't success." - Peta Kelly

I began to ask myself, "What does life want from me?" And as I asked bigger questions, I began getting bigger answers.

Are you living to work or working to live? Ideally, neither! You're stepping into your calling where you can earn well while doing good for yourself and the world!

Have you ever been annoyed by those people who say, "It's not work!" Or thought they were delusional? They were following their hearts, not their resumes.

Follow your heart, find your calling. Our calling is the magic point where who we are meets what we do. A calling is what you work *on*, a title or achievement is what you work *toward*. Which one do you think feels better and creates more impact?

Part of stepping into a calling that allows you to live in your BE state is understanding the difference between your zone of competence, excellence, and genius. It's learning to recognize what comes naturally to you and enhancing it, instead of idolizing what comes easily to others and then enduring imposter syndrome while you attempt to copy their genius.

In Gaye Hendricks's book "The Big Leap," he asks the following questions:

- "What work do you do that doesn't seem like work?"

- "In your work, what produces the highest ratio of abundance and satisfaction to the amount of time spent?"

- "What is your unique ability?"

That doesn't mean it'll always be easy. Resistance will continue to arise. Doing things worthwhile is often about growing through the parts you aren't comfortable with and don't love. But that which calls you, which draws you to it, will pull you past the challenge.

TOOLS FOR *BEING*, #16
WHAT EXCITES YOU?

Perhaps you know exactly what your calling is and you're working joyously on it. Or you're wondering what it could be and why you don't know it.

The questions below will not only give you clarity toward the things that excite you, but are also excellent questions to ask someone when you meet them, instead of "What do you do?"

What excites you right now? _____

_____

_____

What are you grateful for? _____

_____

_____

What are you passionate about? _____

_____

_____

What are you working on? _____

_____

_____

What are you looking forward to? _____

_____

_____

What are you thinking about? _____

_____

_____

What do you like to do? _____

_____

_____

What's the best thing that's happened to you this year? _____

_____

_____

What causes do you support? _____

_____

_____

What is the most interesting thing you've learned recently? _____

_____

_____

What's the most important thing I should know about you? _____

_____

_____

JUST BECAUSE YOU COULD,
DOESN'T MEAN YOU SHOULD.

In 2015, I spent a year studying everything related to health and nutrition, earning a certification in Holistic Health and Integrative Nutrition from the Institute of Integrative Nutrition. I did it because I'm endlessly fascinated with ways to heal the body, with increasing energy and optimization and to better understand toxicity, inflammation, and how to avoid them.

I wasn't interested in working one-on-one with clients on an ongoing basis or becoming a professional nutrition coach. Yet because most of the other students in the program were focused on it, and because I constantly was sharing about health on social media, I often had people asking me for advice.

So many other nutritionists told me how lucky I was to have a network of people following me to learn more about health and who were interested in hiring me. I began to think I "should" take on clients because I could. And finding and booking clients was easy. I was offering my services, and everyone was saying yes. That's abundance, right?

But those appointments started to feel like obligations. I didn't feel relaxed, I felt robotic. I didn't feel joyous, except when the appointment was done. Those clients deserved more. I deserved more. Somewhere, there was someone out there better suited to assist them. They deserved that.

I asked myself, "Is working with health clients one-on-one making me feel relaxed, abundant, and joyous? No." There was my answer!

When you begin to recognize opportunity everywhere, it's easy to want to do everything good that comes your way. In entrepreneurship, the opportunity for collaborations seem to be around every corner, opportunities to create, invitations to speak, clients you could serve. And I'm a yes-girl. But every "yes" is a "no" to something else.

Be abundant in saying no! Taking on a responsibility you don't want is not a badge of honor. You're not only taking away from your ability to create, thrive, and impact, but you're taking away from someone else's ability to experience empowered change and connection.

Give freely of your love, but fiercely protect your energy and time.

TOOLS FOR *BEING*, #17
IF YOU DON'T LOVE WHAT YOU'RE DOING, ASK YOURSELF THIS

1. Is it the place or the role? Is your workplace toxic because of the corporate culture or an unpredictable boss?

If you enjoy the environment and team but not the role you're in, explore opportunities to change to a different project or department. No company wants turnover (it's expensive and time-consuming), so if you're a valued employee, they will likely work with you if there are other opportunities in-house.

The problem *really* is: _____

_____

_____

_____

_____

2. Have you done all you can?

Did you at one point love what you did, but things have changed? If you feel stuck, chances are you aren't giving your all. And if your boss and team are picking up on that (which they very likely are), it's probable you aren't getting all-star treatment or your pick of the most rewarding work.

Before you leave on a sputtering trail of effort, vow to put in *all* of your talent and skill, like when you got hired. Make amends with any office nemesis and act like it's your own organization. Chances are that things might greatly improve and your feelings about work will too. And if they don't, you leave knowing it *really* wasn't you – and likely with a positive recommendation.

What have I done? What else can I do? _____

_____

_____

_____

_____

_____

_____

3. Is the grass greener?

It's possible that another company might offer more vacation time and glitzier holiday parties. But is the day-to-day better than what you're experiencing now? While every company will give you their best face forward in an interview, reach out to your network to find people in the organization who will give you a truthful perspective.

Talk to people who have been there for some time and ask them high-mileage (open-ended) questions, such as what they like best about working there, what changes have they seen that are positive (and negative), and what they would change if they were the boss.

Who can I reach out to? What is really important to me in a place of work? What are my non-negotiables for what I want (vacation time, health insurance, ability to move up)? What will I *not* endure (toxic environments, pay less than _____, long commute time)? _____

_____

_____

_____

_____

_____

_____

_____

_____

4. Are you fulfilling your passion?

Maybe you love your team and company, but find your mind wandering to things that light your heart on fire! Working a job that looks good on paper but doesn't fulfill you can be the slow death of happiness.

Book a consultation with a life or career coach or attend a personal development weekend focused on assisting you in discovering your passions! And when you find it, you can start out with a hobby or side hustle before making the jump, which will allow you to determine if it's the right fit for you. And if it is, that passion is the fuel to make it happen!

When my mind wanders, where does it go? If I could start my career over with any option, what would I be doing? Do I feel my work takes energy or gives me energy? _____

_____

_____

_____

_____

_____

_____

_____

IMPACT

When I die, I don't want to be buried. My remains aren't the physical crumblings of my body. My remains are what I leave behind in memories, in legacy, in impact. It is the people I've touched and how I've inspired them to impact others.

It's the people I've given to, but more importantly, it's the people that I've shown the mission of living to give. Leveraged impact is doing something that multiplies, that takes on a life of its own. Where impact flows until you become redundant, not the founder or the CEO or the change maker. Where you're a channel that impact flowed through, but where you're not needed to keep the flow going.

We are conditioned to be for others. How can you harness this tool?

Life isn't about what you have, it's about what you give. You can give money. You can give time. You can give resources. You can give hope. You can give community.

And in times when I didn't have a lot, it was the generosity of others that made such an impact in my life and in my heart – and created a desire within me to have the same impact.

LIVING TO GIVE

I believe that we live our most abundant lives when we're really coming from a place where we live to give. Not in a way where we put others first out of obligation or martyrdom, but in a way that requires us focusing on being expansive, impactful, and conscious of our connection to those around us. When we are focused on showing up in a way that positively impacts others, it calls us forward to *being* our best selves.

Throughout my life, I've found such joy in giving to others or causes I feel passionate about. Whether it's giving my time to organizations like Court Appointed Special Advocates as a volunteer advocate working with foster youth or donating money to fund pediatric gene research or sponsoring a ride to raise money for cancer research.

The idea of intentionally designing giving into my life and adopting the principle of living to give didn't occur until five years ago. It happened when I was introduced to network marketing. It's a big part of the reason I got over my ego and became open to social marketing as a vehicle for massive impact, and as a result, for financial opportunity.

When I first ordered a 30-day nutritional rebalancing system with Isagenix, my sponsor said, "Hey, you can share these with others and get your products paid for and even earn money." I declined. I had an ego around the idea of network marketing, thinking it was somehow less than my corporate success. And I had excuses that I was too busy to take the time to do the research I thought I needed to do.

Five days incorporating the system into my busy life, I woke up transformed. I couldn't stop talking about how good I felt and sharing with friends about how obsessed I was with how easy it was. I couldn't stop talking about the energy and mental clarity, and I dropped a couple of dress sizes in less than two months. Of course, people noticed. I just didn't really understand that there was a compensation opportunity. I just knew everyone deserves to feel as good as I did!

A few months in, my sponsor, the person that enrolled me, reaching out and saying, "How much money have you earned?"

I wasn't sure what she was talking about.

She said, "Well, how much money have you earned?" I said, "Well, I've got free vitamins twice, so I don't know. I think that's about $280."

She said, "No, not in free products. How much actual money have you earned?"

I didn't really understand I was actually earning real money deposited into a VISA card each week, since I had never even opened the envelope with the card in it! I had told myself a story that I didn't have the time to figure it out. I went and got the card, activated it, and found out there was almost $2,400 on it.

One, it didn't even make sense to me how, after six months of eating food, I could have earned that much when I'd only told a dozen or so people. But I was grateful to receive that money, because even though my ego had a story when I first started I didn't "need" more money, the reality is when the money dropped into my bank account, there were a bunch of things that came to mind I could use it for!

First, I went out and bought a $500 Pottery Barn rug for my patio that I just could not justify to myself otherwise! I had been telling myself, "I'm not spending $500 for an outdoor rug." But guess what? With an extra $2,400, I absolutely did.

The second thing is what opened my mind up and ultimately changed my entire life. My friend Amanda was a new mom and was going through cancer treatment. Her family had set up a GoFundMe page for her because she had to quit her job and drop out of her Ph.D. program to focus on getting better. The situation was unimaginable.

For several months, I had donated $100. I felt good about helping but each month I'd donate money, I'd think how much I'd like to be giving more. It wasn't that I couldn't give more, it was that I couldn't give more without changing my lifestyle.

When I discovered this $2,400 of extra income, I thought, "I want to give Amanda $500 this month." I donated $500 to her GoFundMe, and a couple of days later, she reached out to me and told me that she cried when she received it. They'd been praying for this extra money and it helped them make it through their month, but also it helped her do treatment at home with her boys. It moved me to tears because I could tell in her voice what it meant to her.

I thought, "Wait a second. I used products that made me feel incredible and would tell anybody about because I feel so good! I couldn't stop sharing if I tried because I know how many people are struggling to feel good. I received a thank-you bonus because I opened my mouth and then I was able to turn around and give more money and impact someone I care about." It was a circle of giving and receiving and I wanted more of it.

THE GO-GIVER

This became even more tangible when soon after I read **The Go-Giver: A Little Story About a Powerful Business Idea**. It's about business principles that apply everywhere in life and it's about learning how to shift our focus from getting to giving, which means constantly providing value to others. My first time reading it, I read it twice on the same day.

1. The Law Of Value

Your true worth is determined by how much more you give in value than you take in payment. The key to this is understanding the difference between price and value. Price is a dollar amount. Value is the relative worth to the person receiving it.

In business, money is just an echo of value. Value must come first, and then the money is the result we get from what we've provided. The more we focus on the value, the more money will come.

2. The Law Of Compensation

Our income is determined by how many people we serve and how well we serve them. This is where we look at the importance of really impacting large numbers of people. This is about working smarter, not harder, because there are people out there who are working incredibly hard, maybe doing manual jobs, farm work, digging ditches, and they're working their butts off, but they're not being paid very much. At the same time, how many people are they impacting?

The question to ask is, how can I serve more people and make sure there are no limits? Because if there is a limit on how many people you can serve, then there is always going to be a limit on how much you can earn. The law of compensation represents actual income, and the rule is:

Exceptional Value + Significant Reach = High Compensation.

3. The Law Of Influence

Your influence is determined by how abundantly you place other people's interests first, and when you do so correctly, it can result in a really big win for everyone involved. I like to think that when we focus on ourselves, when we put our own interests first, it causes us to move really slowly, to get stuck or even move backward at times. Zig Ziglar once said, "Help others achieve what they want and it'll help you achieve what you want." That's a powerful lesson to learn.

There's this golden rule of business, which is that all things being equal, people will do business and refer business to people they know, like, and trust. The fastest way to success is actually focusing on others.

4. The Law of Authenticity

The most valuable gift we have to offer is ourselves, that you have exactly what it takes to add great value to the world and just live a genuinely happy and successful life. That first happens when you show up as yourself consistently.

I want you to understand that you don't need to *learn* to be authentic, you just need to embrace being yourself. We're often putting on these masks because we feel like we need to show up as a perfect person or a better version of ourselves instead of really being authentic. That doesn't mean get online and whine all day, but it means it's okay to show people you're imperfect.

At a recent event, the life coach for both Oprah and for Robert Downey, Jr. shared this idea. He said, "Your message is your mess, or let your mess be your message." It boils down to being authentic, because you never know who you're going to impact with who you are or what you're going through.

5. The Law Of Receptivity

Some people say, "I'm really good at giving but I'm not good at receiving." I used to be guilty of this as well. But breathe for a moment. Breathe out, and then in, and then out, and then in. You can't do one without the other. You can't breathe out without first breathing in, or vice versa, right? There's no breathing out without breathing in, and giving and receiving works the same way. It works best together.

There are times you're going to focus on the giving, but by being open to receiving, you are going to receive some incredible things. The more you give, the more you receive, so make sure you are receiving what the universe is trying to give you so you'll continue to have more to give back.

GIVE DAY, PAY DAY

I have created the practice of giving or tithing 10% of my income. It doesn't matter how much you earn; it's about giving regardless of the amount. It's getting in that practice of giving so you open yourself up to receiving. I encourage you to do a payday give day. Whatever day you get paid, give back a percentage of that gross amount. That will keep you in that give-and-receive state of abundance!

☐ Check It Off. What's a cause you'd love to donate to? If you don't have one top of mind, do you have someone you love who has a cause you can support? Set up an automatic payment for a percentage of your income the day you get paid! Even if it's 1%, it's setting up that circle of abundance!

My friend Chris Harder says, "When good people earn good money, they do great things."

TOOLS FOR *BEING*, #18
HOW TO CREATE IMPACT

Bi-monthly income: _____

Percentage or dollar amount you'd like to give _____

What impact will your gift create? Make it tangible! _____

_____

_____

How will you *feel* in giving? _____

_____

_____

Another wonderful habit is to donate a percentage of your time. What does that look like? That could be volunteering for a non-profit, supporting a local cause, or even donating your time in a mentorship program. I love spending 5-10% of my time mentoring female entrepreneurs who are not yet in the financial position to hire a coach.

One way to ensure you spend a substantial amount of time volunteering is to tie it in to travel! Spend a half day or full day on your trip giving back to a local organization wherever you're visiting! It'll make you more aware of the area and culture outside of the typical tourist pursuits, plus give you an added appreciation for the abundance in your life to be able to vacation!

Twice a year, before our annual Isagenix business development conferences, we spend half a day giving our time to a local charity. We've volunteered at food banks preparing meal boxes and hygiene kits, helping to feed 17,000 people that week. We've cleaned sleeping mats and organized supplies in the largest homeless shelter in San Antonio. And at the events themselves, millions are raised for causes to impact lives around the globe.

Though we come from all over the world, we are united by a common desire to create a legacy of contribution, to be part of something bigger than ourselves and to lift others up in the process. I couldn't be more grateful to have found a community whose values align with mine, whose mission inspires me into action, and where everyone's hand is a helping hand.

We all have time and can all create time. We all have the same 24 hours in the day that Oprah and Beyonce do. Look at how much they give. And when you're focused on the creation of a positive output like giving, you'll prioritize it over the less important commitments that may not be moving you forward to who you want to be.

TOOLS FOR *BEING*, #19
TIME TO GIVE

☐ Check It Off. Where can you schedule in one or two hours per month to give back? Can you do this with a spouse, friend, or business partner to not only multiply the impact, but also to create quality time in your highest energetic state with someone you care about?

Community Service or Community Give Back

_____

_____

Business mentorship or providing emotional support

_____

_____

Note to yourself: When you focus on giving, be open to what you're receiving back! Gratitude, appreciation, feeling impactful!

The third practice I encourage you to consider is asking people, "What would be a helpful introduction for you in business or life?" It's so easy to tell people what you're doing, but when you meet someone, try asking, "Hey, what would be helpful for you? What are your goals right now, and what would be a helpful introduction or resource that could help you?"

If you're referring them to someone else, you're actually going to be helping two people. If you're referring them to a resource, you're helping them. In the end, it is all about living to give.

TOOLS FOR *BEING*, #20
PAYING IT FORWARD

☐ Check It Off. Who are five people you know in a referral job (contractors, salespeople, realtors, network marketers)? Or someone looking for a new job, funds, or help? Who are five people you know who currently need what they offer? Make an introduction with no expectations except connecting good people! Or give people a resource (a book, podcast, or tool) that you know could help them!

#1 Introduction or tool:

#2 Introduction or tool:

#3 Introduction or tool:

#4 Introduction or tool:

#5 Introduction or tool:

Note to yourself: Make it your goal to leave every conversation or new meeting with giving an introduction, tool, or referral that is helpful to the other person!

CHAPTER 10

Always Be Growing

"The swiftest way to triple your success is
to double your investment in personal development."
– ROBIN SHARMA

When you're in your BE state, it feels like magic is happening. You're aligned with your best self. People show up. Opportunity shows up. It's easy to feel open when you're in that place.

And as much as it's vital that we learn the ingredients that create magic in our life, like growth, collaboration, self-care, and impact, it's also vital that we understand those that tend to dull the magic.

MINDSET

We've all heard of the phrase "quality of life." It's a mix of our health, our finances, our freedom, our relationships, and our time, the building blocks of how well we live and how happy we are. But what if the quality of life is actually determined by the quality of our mind? By our mindset?

Mindset is our most valuable resource, more than our health, our finances, our time, our relationships? Why? Because it dictates all of the other resources, as well as how resourceful we are. The BE state you choose to live in *is* the descriptive of your mindset. You're just giving it a name.

Our mind is *the* most powerful tool we possess, and our mindset is the way we receive and filter all of the inputs we receive in our experience. And like choosing what we nourish our body with, we also have the responsibility and privilege of selecting much of what we feed our mind that alters our mindset.

Robin Sharma says, "What we focus on grows, what you think about expands, and what you dwell upon determines your destiny."

If you've studied the Law of Attraction, the idea is that thoughts contain energy, and like a magnet, they will attract similar energies together. So positive thoughts will bring positive thoughts, people, or experiences to you, while negative thoughts will attract negative thoughts, people, or experiences.

More than a decade before I was first introduced to the Law of Attraction by the movie *The Secret*, I had taken a class in high school called Peer Helpers. It was the seed for personal development I would begin to intentionally explore a decade later. The concept of mindset was *such* a simple idea, but also so powerful when I began to understand that our thoughts, our mindset, controls everything.

What I learned was broken down into four concepts:

Good situations + Good Thoughts = Good Outcome

Good Situations + Bad Thoughts = Bad Outcome

Bad situations + Bad Thoughts = Bad Outcome

Bad Situations + Good Thoughts = Good Outcome

Simply stated, the way we think about anything we experience will result in a more positive outcome. Or: whether you think something is good or bad, you're right.

So what are you doing to improve your quality of mindset? The mindset that decides what you'll do each day, how you'll act, how you'll receive things, and how you'll treat others?

Meditation? Affirmations? Visualization? Self-care? Coaching? Reading?

What's the recipe for your best quality of mind? For your BE state? In your BE state, it's unlikely you're overeating or making poor choices.

ARE YOU STARVING OR FEEDING YOUR MIND (AND LIFE)

One of the most powerful concepts I learned from the Institute for Integrative Nutrition was the concept of "primary foods." These aren't the things we fill our plates with, but are the bigger ingredients in our life that include the people around us, how we choose to spend our time, how we move our bodies, and more. They are what feed our mind, our energy, our souls.

Institute for Integrative Nutrition Primary Foods - spiritual connection, love and relationships, physical activity, career and finances.

TOOLS FOR *BEING*, #21
THE PRIMARY FOODS OF
YOUR LIFE

On a scale from 1 to 10, one being almost non-existent and 10 being *incredible*, how do you feel about these areas of primary foods in your life?

- Spiritual Connection _____
- Love and Relationships _____
- Physical Activity _____
- Career and Finances _____

When we aren't nourishing our lives properly with our primary foods, it creates "emotional hunger." According to author Dr. Michael Gershon, who wrote "Our Second Brain" about nerve cells in the gut acting as a brain for our gut, when we are happy, fulfilled, and engaged in what we are doing, we have little need for food beyond what will sustain us and keep us functional.

When we are emotionally hungry, because we haven't fulfilled ourselves with the proper "primary foods," we attempt to feed that hunger physically, often with unhealthy choices. So before starting a diet, take an inventory of your life and primary foods to identify the causes of that emotional hunger. The chances of succeeding with any positive changes you're desiring will be so much higher if you're first addressing your level of connection, your movement, and with whom (and how) you are spending your time.

Your BE state check-in questions will assist you in guiding you toward a life (and plate) full of primary foods (and actual foods) that nourish you!

Check In: Does this choice/food/activity allow me to feel _____ (BE state).

A HAPPY MEAL - FOR YOUR MINDSET

What will you choose to nourish your mind with today? What are the ingredients for the healthiest, most abundant mindset?

For me, it's not reading the news in the morning, but instead, feeding my mind with inspiration. That could be an affirmation recording, uplifting music, listening to a thought leader, or a motivating podcast. While breakfast may be the most important meal for our body to set the tone of the day, what we start our day with mentally lays the foundation for the rest of the day's intake and output of experience. And it affects the choices of what you nourish your body with!

I used to wake up (after hitting the snooze several times) and grab my phone from the bedside table, already stressing out about what e-mails I needed to answer and what appointments I had that day. It was a recipe for killing the morning vibes!

If the first thing you do in the morning is grab your phone and start scrolling social media or checking your text messages, you're giving yourself a serious dose of cortisol in the morning! I've never seen an improvement in my mood by doing either in the morning!

My personal goal each morning is to complete my morning routine, or power hour, before I touch the phone. In fact, I leave it in the kitchen so I'm not tempted (and not exposing myself to extra electromagnetic fields that can interfere with sleep).

That extra 20-30 minutes of meditation, gratitudes, reading, and planning out my day (while sipping on tea) not only sets my day up for massive success by creating the foundation of a healthy mindset, but it somehow slows time down!

Your mind and mindset are muscles. If we don't use them, they get weak. So invest a little time each morning in feeding your mind before you feed your body.

 In Chapter 12 Tools For Being You , you'll find more information on the ingredients to create a happy meal for your mindset!

FEAR

Let's talk about fear. I believe that when we need to hear something and we are really open, we hear whatever it is that we require to grow through what we're going through. In August 2019, I attended a personal development event where it seemed as if every single speaker was talking about fear, and fear is the reason I almost canceled going to the event in the first place. That fear stemmed from taking Valentina with me.

The week prior, we had gone on a road trip up to Oregon and the first two nights were incredibly rough.

She was out of her routine with the travel and it was incredibly hot and uncomfortable. Each night, she cried for nearly two hours while I rocked her, tried unsuccessfully to nurse her, and all the other mama tools to calm her down and get her to sleep.

I experienced a moment of total overwhelm and desperation, where she was crying and Luca was clinging to my leg, begging for mommy, when I lost it. In that moment of total frustration and breastfeeding hormones, I looked at my husband and cried, "I want to walk away from my life."

After those two nights, even though the next couple of days were easy breezy, and she was back to her normal, calm, happy baby self, I was petrified to take her by myself from Oregon to Nashville. I was focusing on those worst-case scenarios, afraid that the trip would not only be miserable, but questioning if I was a bad mom for putting her into a situation that could be upsetting her from her normal routine.

But I needed to go to that event. I knew it would catapult me forward. It would restrict my fire of being excited about building my business, and not just my network marketing business, but all of my businesses. Every year, this event is just what lights my life on fire to be more and to do more. It just fills up my passion cup.

If it weren't for the women that I was going with, the women that I would be staying with, I wouldn't have gone. It would've been so much easier not to go.

It seemed as if *every* speaker on stage was talking about their struggles and how they had fear about doing the hard things to change it. And then, they would talk about the incredible things that happened when they got on the other side of fear.

The keynote speaker, Michelle Poler, spoke entirely about *fear*. She had committed to a 100-day project where she faced a fear every day. These fears range from skydiving to cliff diving to letting spiders crawl on her and culminated in facing her fear of public speaking by doing a TEDx on the 100th day.

She said something about fear that really stuck with me. That explained that fear is our ally, but only if we really understand it so we know its purpose.

There are three categories of fear.

First, universal fear. This is the fear that keeps us safe, that keeps us alive. It encompasses fear of heights, such as not falling off a cliff, so we don't die. That fear is okay, it's our true ally.

Then there's cultural fear, the fear that keeps us from being outliers. It's the fear of not being loved or being accepted. This is a fear that really hurts our ability to live authentically as us because it keeps us from being our *true* selves.

Last, there's personal fear, which is what keeps us from being our *best* selves. It keeps us from reaching our potential. That fear is often what causes us choose Netflix and chilling over finishing that project that we know can help us realize a dream that we've had. It's the fear that keeps us small.

Michelle stated that "the enemy of success isn't failure. It is comfort." That hit home for me. What we want the most is the scariest. It's what we have most fear around.

In my life at times when I've been really bold or when I've been out there doing things, I have people that say, "Oh, you're not afraid of anything." That couldn't be further from the truth. I'm afraid of a lot of things, but there's a difference between being fearless and being brave.

When I've done things in my life that I was scared of, I was being brave. I wasn't being fearless. When I stood up and did my TEDx speech, I was pretty sure as I was smiling that my teeth were rattling and that people could hear it because I was terrified.

I have learned that when I am terrified and I do it anyway, that is where the growth happens. That's where my growth zone or my zone of discomfort grows, and all of the best things come out of that! The first few times

I flew with both of my children, I was terrified. I had crippling anxiety. I did it anyway, and everything was ok.

I want you to understand that both fear and courage are a part of us, but we choose which one we let tip of the scale. Are we so allowing our fear to be so heavy in our lives that our courage is just a little tiny thing? Instead of asking yourself what is the worst that can happen, Michelle Poler said, ask yourself what is the *best* that could happen.

On the trip to Nashville, when I was thinking about not going, I asked myself, "What's the worst that can happen?" The worst that could happen was lots of crying, me being tired in the morning from a rough night, and the mom guilt that asks, "Am I doing the best thing for my child if I'm putting her in a state where she cries?"

When I asked what's the best that can happen? Supporting incredible women that have a desire to change their lives, the lives of their families, and SO many more.

And I realized, when the more I help others, the better my life gets. It's not because my income grows, though it does. I'm so grateful and appreciative for that, because one, that allows me to have more abundance in my life, to give more abundantly, and to have more choice.

When I help others, my impact grows as my income grows. The more I help others, the more I'm living in my purpose. *That* is where I get happiness from. That's where I'm allowed to be more.

So I knew that facing that *personal* fear was so worth it. And I was right.

My question for you: are you showing up for your dreams bravely? Are you honoring them, or are you letting fear get in the way?

Have courage, because everything you want to be and do and have is just on the other side of fear.

GROWING THROUGH IT

How often do you hear "you'll get over it"? As if it's just a hill to climb and then we're on the other side. The reality of a challenge, of a struggle, or of pain, is that when we crest that hill, we see more, feel more. We'll never be the same because we've experienced something we hadn't before.

We don't get *over* something, we get *through* it. The journey will have highs and lows, but the importance is moving forward, even if it's at different elevations and different speeds. And sometimes, moving forward requires a detour or even a step back.

And ideally, we *grow* through it. When we struggle, it changes us. We don't have a choice in that. But we do choose how we perceive it, how we act upon it and HOW it changes us.

Do we retract or expand? As we move forward, use it to *grow*. Keep going, keep growing.

DO YOU NEED TO CHANGE YOUR EXPECTATIONS?

Happiness occurs when our expectations equal our situation.

How often are you creating expectations that are impossible to meet? If we base our expectations on the way things should look on the highlight reel of social media or the curated photos on Pinterest without really grounding ourselves into what is important to us, we are setting ourselves up for constant disappointment.

I remember when Luca turned two and could participate in Saturday soccer, I was so excited to take him! He'd loved kicking balls at gym class, so I was sure he'd love soccer. As we drove to his first practice, I laughed at myself that at 37, it was my first "soccer mom" moment.

My vision of him happily kicking away at the ball lasted about three minutes. The remaining 27 minutes he ran *fast*, the opposite direction of his little group. He was far more interested in the retirees doing tai chi than any organized activities. And for a few minutes, I was disappointed. Why? Because I had an expectation I had fantasized about and the situation wasn't living up to the expectations.

And then I gave myself a reality check that the day wasn't about soccer, it was about doing something as a family. It was about Luca enjoying himself. It was about being outside with the two I love the most, enjoying the weather. It was about making memories of life, not perfection. So I changed my expectation.

We headed nearby to the playground, went down slides with him, and had *such* a blast. And it showed me that I can have that every day by being open to the magic of the moment, focusing on my BE state, and being positively realistic about my expectations.

When you're not experiencing what you want, you either need to reset your expectations or your effort. And by focusing on how you want to feel, on your BE state instead of what you need to *do* or *have*, you can meet and exceed those expectations more and more.

TOOLS FOR *BEING,* #22
EXPECTATIONS

Think of a recent situation that upset or disappointed you. What were your expectations going into it?

_____

_____

_____

How could you have found or experienced the feelings of your BE state within the situation without anything changing?

_____

_____

_____

Think of an event coming up that you are excited to experience or be part of! What do you expect out of it?_____

_____

_____

_____

How could your expectations guarantee you'll experience joy or happiness as part of it? _____

_____

_____

_____

PUSHING YOUR TRIGGER POINTS ON PURPOSE

Do you have certain things that trigger you? A situation, a smell, a word that sends you into a spiral, a freak-out, or just generally takes you in the opposite direction from your BE state? What do you do about it? You avoid it!

What is a trigger point? It's a fear – perhaps of failure, or of our significant other repeating a pattern of something an ex did, or a word that brings us back to a time that we were traumatized.

What triggers me? Having someone question my intentions (my previous response was to ignore them or cut them out of life); criticism (I used to become defensive). The last natural thing we do when someone hits a trigger point is dig a little deeper. We go into fight or flight (run from it or fight it).

Why we need to stop avoiding our triggers and face them with trigger point training?

Trigger point training/flexibility builds connection to areas of your body so you can key into a muscle and relax it deliberately (just like we contract it). It's a trainable skill, the ability to be so engaged that you can focus in on it and let it go.

Translated: by facing those fears or triggers, we can build the strength to not let it affect us. Just like we can think about a situation and get mentally and emotionally keyed up, we also can build the ability to be in a triggered situation and mentally and emotionally master our feelings.

What does ignoring it do? It creates a trigger point sensitivity, making the structure behave differently. This causes the body to compensate by having muscles around it do things they shouldn't, or ones that should, stop working properly. Basically, you get more messed up.

Working through it can be highly painful, so go slow. Embrace the worst areas, don't avoid the worst areas. In fact, search for the worst areas, because that is where the biggest global impact will be created. If you find the epicenter of these things and get them to release, you get body-wide instant benefits. You get them to release through repeated trigger point practice.

The result? It's totally comfortable to put pressure on what *used* to be trigger points. It just feels like a little pressure. The end goal isn't to have a trigger point-free body, it's that it ceases to impact how you move through life and how you feel.

How do you work them? You hire a professional who shows you the tools to do the work. With physical trigger points, you work with a skilled trainer or physical therapist. In my mindset, I have used coaches for years to increase my awareness of myself and equip myself with tools for a more positive, productive life! Now I'm working with an incredible psychologist because there were a few triggers I couldn't work through with coaches and self-help books.

She's using tools (like EMDR, an interactive psychotherapy technique used to relieve psychological stress) to help me rewire these triggers and showing me how to use them myself, so I can break through those trigger points and build the strength to not let them affect me.

My end goal is not to say nothing triggers me. I's just to cease letting those old triggers impact how I move through life and how I feel.

TOOLS FOR *BEING*, #23
DEFINING YOUR TRIGGERS

What triggers you? What causes you to shut down, fight, or flee?

_____

_____

_____

What is your natural response? _____

_____

_____

_____

What does that cost you? _____

_____

_____

_____

How would you like to respond that would be aligned with your BE state? _____

_____

_____

_____

What resources could you use to change your response? _____
_____
_____
_____

HOW TO CURE AN EMOTIONAL HANGOVER

We are all familiar with the concept of hangover.

It's when you have too many drinks and the next day, you feel less than your best. Perhaps a headache, fatigue, crankiness, and nausea. Why? Because alcohol disrupts sleep, dehydrates you, and usually leads to less willpower.

Unlike alcohol, an emotional hangover is harder to avoid.

What is it?

An emotional hangover is when you are exposed to something that creates a lasting emotional effect or imprint. It can often cause bad dreams and you wake up with anxiety, dread, worry, or don't even want to get out of bed. Or you go through your day anxious and depressed, and suddenly, more and more seems to be going wrong. Why? Because where focus flows, energy goes. What you focus on expands, what you focus on grows.

What causes it?

- TV! Reality TV, scary or violent movies, or things that are really troubling, and we often watch TV right before bed, which means our subconscious is trying to work through it. Instead of our own challenges, our subconscious is using its resources to try to solve fictional ones!

- Consuming too much news with a focus on the "world is falling apart."

- An interaction with someone who is negative, passive aggressive, or who triggers you.

- A job you detest

To cure it, change your state! Emotional hangovers will last as long as we allow them. There are so many options that can cure that emotional hangover quickly, but it begins with deciding to change it instead of wallowing in it!

EMOTIONAL HANGOVER REMEDIES:

- **Meditate**. Clear the mental air and quiet the noise.

- **Practice Gratitude**. Gratitude is the medicine that treats anxiety!

- **Exercise**. Get your body moving. When blood flows, energy flows.

- **Get Outside**. Vitamin D, blue skies, and fresh air help ground us and reprioritize things.

- **Eat Healthy**. Eating poorly isn't going to improve how you feel.

- **Be creative or joyous**. This gives you perspective, and joy is a powerful antidote.

- **Take action**. Stop spinning your mental wheels. Especially if the hangover is from something that made you feel disempowered, remind yourself of all of the ways you own your life.

TOOLS FOR *BEING*, #24
CREATE A LIST OF ANTIDOTES

Note when you feel anxious, negative, withdrawn, or pessimistic. How did you spend your time prior to that? What activities did you take part in? _____

_____

_____

_____

What will snap you out of it? Create a remedy list or menu of antidotes!

_____

_____

_____

Does this mean you'll never do anything or be exposed to anything that gives you an emotional hangover? Unlikely! But it's about *being* aware!

WHO YOU'LL BECOME

Cars, houses, investments. They can all be taken away. But what can't be is the person you'll become.

I lost it all. And I would do it again to get where I am today. To a state that doesn't require a lot of things (though I appreciate the abundance), to a state where someone else's opinion of me doesn't dictate my self-worth or my value.

To be in a BE state of power within, rather than a *do* state that requires an outside conflict.

In my early 20s, when I did some modeling, I had a photographer tell me he'd never photograph me because of the birthmark on my face. That same year, a co-worker spread rumors that my boyfriend hit me and it was a bruise.

That birthmark had been part of me since I was conceived. I only thought of it when I was sick (because it would turn bright red when I was pale). I never had shame around it and somehow made it through school without ever being teased. I never tried to cover it up.

After those comments, I became self-conscious. It seemed so much bigger when I looked at it. I developed a "favorite side" of my face, where I'd turn to minimize my "flawed" side. I covered it up or photoshopped it in photos. I had photo facials in my mid-20s, hoping it would lighten.

When I met my husband, I told him I planned to laser it off when I could take time off from work. He told me he loved it, and it made me unique and not to do it. I met with a dermatologist anyway, though they told me it was unlikely they could lighten it or remove it, given the type it was. It's one time I'm *really* fortunate that I didn't have the time off work.

My journey to becoming an entrepreneur involved as much self growth and self-love as it did learning strategy, branding, and business growth. In fact, in entrepreneurship, your business income and success usually only grow as much as you grow as a person.

As I built a social selling business, I learned over time to not care (or to care less) what the negative people out there said. They were the same people that were looking for my flaws, to point them out and tear me down. It took putting myself out there more to realize the stones stopped hurting after a few were thrown.

Instead, I focused on the people who supported me, the people who found beauty in my imperfections, physically and emotionally, who were open-minded enough to ask lovingly why I'd leave a successful corporate career for something outside the box. In the same way that I focus on the people who will ask me, "Oh, is that a bruise?" I can respond, "Nope, it's my birthmark," with no story of being flawed tied to it. It's just a part of me.

Now, I don't have a good side. I face the camera straight on because ME encompasses all of me. I'm one of a kind, and I'm proud to be me. And you should be, too. There's no physical difference in my birthmark. There's only the mindset shift.

A shift in mindset may not look like anything. It doesn't have to be a life changing "a-ha" moment. But the ability for a change in mindset to be more open, more abundant, and more possible to change your life will be more impactful than any amount in your bank account or any connection that could happen. Your mindset will be your most valuable asset and everything you receive will be a reflection of the health of it.

CHAPTER 11

Being In Love And Relationships

"The best thing to hold onto in life is each other."
– AUDREY HEPBURN

One morning, I was on a call with a beautiful energy life coach from the UK and she said something that resonated to my core. She said, "You are the center of your universe."

We are taught to always give, give, give and not to put ourselves first. We are told taking care of our own needs is selfish. And many jobs in corporate America reward the "work till you drop" mentality.

Where is this different? When you're on an airplane with a child, they remind you in case of emergency to put on your air mask before assisting your child. The reality is that if we don't put ourselves first in terms of filling our cup, of loving ourselves, of nourishing ourselves, we have so much less to give. Fill that cup.

We are the center of our universe. How big and bright that universe is entirely depends upon *you*.

BE YOU FIRST

I've often been told I'm *too* intense. That I do *too* much. That I want *too* much.

For years, I wavered between trying to stifle my passion, my emotions, and my dreams to match the expectations of others, to be more "chill," to come across with a cool indifference. The only thing I succeeded in was feeling untrue to myself.

And at other times, I pushed aside the other voices and danced to my own tune! And that is when I was uniquely me. That is when my heart soared, when I'd just hug people because I felt like it (or felt like they needed it), when I bought the red shoes, when I'd dance with the belly dancers at a restaurant or ask the bongo drummer if I could take a turn. That, my friends, is when memories were made and when I was *me*.

In the past few years, those other voices have quieted until they are only a memory. A memory to remind me that living in my brilliance isn't just for me, but to give permission to all of the women and girls out there who may want to get up and sing karaoke or hold the boa constrictor in science class but are afraid to be themselves.

Don't be what is expected, comfortable or safe. Be you.

MAYBE, IT IS ABOUT YOU

In my third trimester with my baby girl, I was very frustrated. I was about to launch my podcast and I was feeling a lot of fear around putting myself out there and being vulnerable. I hadn't been prioritizing my workouts and I was not sleeping at all. Overall, I felt miserable and really stressed out.

One night my husband got home, and I told him, "I am not feeling supported. I need more support from you." He very calmly told me, "If you're not feeling supported, is there an area of your life you can better support yourself?" In my super tired, moody state, that wasn't exactly what I wanted to hear, but it landed on my heart.

I thought about it and I asked myself: how can I better support me? Am I setting myself up to succeed in the areas that are important to me before I can expect someone else to? I realized was that I was tired, I was stressed, and I was probably a little hungry as well, because I was eight and a half months pregnant.

When we really look honestly at ourselves, we can determine what we need to do to feel supported, or to feel happy, or to feel loved.

The next day I made sure I got some sleep, that I moved my body, nourished myself well, did self-care, and I took care of a couple of the things that were giving me anxiety. And guess what? I felt so much better, and I was super happy with my husband, though he had done nothing differently. And I realized it really was all about me.

It drove home for me the realization that in those moments when we're not feeling supported or not feeling loved, it really does start with us. We have the ability to change it. If you aren't supporting yourself, loving yourself, or happy with yourself, and you're expecting others to fill up your cup, it's like pouring water into a cup with holes in it. There's never going to be enough to fill it up.

When I'm really supporting myself, I am high-vibing on life. I feel support from those around me. It feels like opportunities are falling from the sky!

One morning, I had a little bit of a rough start to the morning. Recognizing I could either go through the day arguing for why it wasn't a great day or

I could stop and support myself, I chose the latter. I meditated, nourishing my body to help support me into feeling my best and practiced gratitudes. I felt so much better, back in my ideal BE state of relaxed, abundant and joyous.

Within the next few hours, two different people reached out to ask me for speaking engagements.

I marveled at the change in the day, at the abundance that was showing up! How had things shifted so quickly? When you're supporting yourself and you're feeling and being your best, there's no room for negativity. There's no room for drama, and people can sense it. It's like you're bulletproof to b.s.

It's your job to support yourself, to make yourself happy, to love yourself before you can expect others to do that. Think about how you can apply this every day to what you're doing, to what you're eating, to the decisions you're making. When you feel supported and happy from within, you're going to feel it from everywhere else. And when you're happy, you can do anything. It's your job to BE first!

BEING OK NOT BEING FOR EVERYONE

It's possible that when you meet someone, they aren't in their BE state. Bad days are caused by many reasons and everyone has them.

But when you meet people, listen to your intuition.

How often did you feel *instantly* comfortable with someone who grows to be a lifelong friend? On the flipside, that person who gave you a negative vibe you couldn't put your finger on – did you ever find out they were secretly someone you totally connected with?

Sometimes, it's even before you've met. It's that meeting you have with a potential client whose e-mail tone was brusque, but you chalked it up to not being able to read personality over e-mail.

While we don't want to prejudge, and we do learn from relationships from those different from us, fundamentally, some people are going to take us out of our BE state. It's not our job to befriend or save everyone, especially at the expense of yourself.

I had a girl reach out to me, asking me to connect. While this happens occasionally, there was something about the exchange that made me feel "off" and the opposite of my calm, abundant, and joyous BE state.

We had a quick phone chat about setting up a time to meet in person to see if we might be able to collaborate on some future projects. I instantly knew, as I listened to her talk, that this was not a person whose energy mixed well with mine.

Instead of feeling relaxed, abundant, and joyous, I felt guarded, grated, and questioning, not only questioning her motives, but questioning if listening to myself, if cutting off a possible relationship before it began, made me a *mean* girl. My former people-pleaser still shows her face now and again.

I found myself waking up daily, expecting a late-night text from her, a text that I would judge by the tone or hour, a text that would make me question why it bothered me, which would bother me. And then I'd have a mental inner battle of whether or not I would respond, how short my answer would be, or if I should make another attempt to set a boundary to extinguish conversation.

It didn't matter my response, any communication left me feeling unsettled. I decided to listen to my intuition and remove the energy from the relationship.

Is there someone in your life who is constantly draining your energetic well? That a text message or contact from creates an instant cortisol spike of stress? Do you continue to tell yourself that there's no real reason for this? Or to give them the benefit of the doubt?

Remember, every time you say yes to someone, you say no to someone else. What space is that person holding that could be available to someone more aligned, or even to deepening your relationship with yourself?

THREE QUESTIONS TO GROW THROUGH PAIN AND HURT

Three simple questions that could have saved me so much time, energy and grief. Three questions that can help you learn, grow, and move past negative emotions that are stopping you from living your best life.

If you feel like you're sensitive and you are getting hurt often...

If you wonder if your current relationships are really serving you and want to give yourself permission to select relationships that serve you and where you want to go in life.

Or if you just want to turn bad weeks or days into bad moments.

Let's be real, we're not always going to be happy. We're not always going to be living a conflict or drama-free life, but we can control how much of our life we are spending in a state outside of our ideal BE state.

Life gives us so many different situations where we feel hurt, criticized, or rejected. With the strong impact social media has on our lives, it's easy to feel hurt or irritated by a comment or message or to feel left out of something.

When you begin to change, whether it's digging into personal development or getting the courage to work on that entrepreneurial idea or side gig, it can be really easy to feel criticized by people who may not understand what we're doing or even be threatened by it.

And if you're in a relationship that doesn't make you feel good, that doesn't allow you to be in your ideal BE state, you're probably feeling frustrated, rejected, or just in an emotional state of low vibration.

When I went full time in my network marketing business after leaving corporate America, I bought into the idea that I had to feel phenomenal *all* the time. If I didn't, I somehow wasn't being true to the state of euphoria I first felt as I transitioned into the entrepreneur life of building my own schedule and designing my life.

I had a situation in my business where someone did something that really felt very violating to me. I got so busy feeling violated that it energetically took me out of my business for weeks, if not months. I was emotionally and mentally absent. I was not in an energetic state where I was going to be attracting business partners or customers.

I couldn't stop obsessing over the situation and it made me feel so stuck. And what we focus on expands. I was talking to other people about how I felt, and in supporting me and my feelings of violation, it gave the situation more energy. It also made me feel right, but just because you feel right, doesn't mean that it's going to fix the situation. It was a really negative situation, and at that time, I didn't have the tools to learn the lesson I later learned. I even spent so much time and money with coaches and with other people trying to get past the situation, instead of getting through it.

And now I want to give you a tool that I created for myself.

TOOLS FOR *BEING*, #25
LESSONS LEARNED

1. What is the lesson to be learned here?

    *   There's always a lesson, especially when we're taking radical responsibility for our experience.

2. Have I learned a lesson? Am I feeling it? Do I understand what to do with it?

    *   So often we realize there's a lesson to be learned, but we're still frustrated or angry. And so though we objectively realized there's a lesson, we really aren't ready to learn the lesson. We're not ready to feel it. We're not ready to move past it.

3. Is there any benefit to feeling this way any longer?

    *   That's when we understand the lesson. We have felt it, we know what we need to do, but we're still choosing to feel violated, hurt, or upset, and not ready to move on.

Bonus question: does this interaction or does this relationship allow me to live in my BE state?

The situation that actually led me to realize all of these questions was a hard one. I had a friend who had been in my life for decades. I considered her one of my best friends. There had been several instances where she'd cut off communication and I didn't know why. And in avoiding conflict, never asked once she began speaking to me again.

This time, it was shortly after miscarrying that I realized it had been months since we'd talked. I wasn't sure why. I had texted her, sent her a couple of e-mails, and left a voicemail, but wasn't getting a response back. I was racking my brain trying to figure out what I did. What did I say that had made her upset or hurt? Or what was it that she had just cut off contact? I had no idea.

I finally reached out, saying, "I obviously did something that really upset you and I don't know what it is. And for me to be able to learn and grow from this, I would really appreciate it if you would let me know."

When she finally broke the silence, I learned that she was upset that I had been moving too fast in the friendship. She felt rushed. Scheduled in. She didn't feel like I was honoring the friendship, that it wasn't a two-way street.

So I thought about it and asked myself the first question: what was the lesson to learn? I was at a point in my life where I was trying to juggle a lot as a full-time mom and a full-time business owner. Doing all of these things at once was really a recipe for disaster.

I actually realized that I was doing too much, and I needed to leverage help. I was trying to do it all, and I was doing none of it well. So I was scheduling my phone calls but then running late, and that's what she'd experienced the last couple of times we'd talked, feeling rushed and unappreciated.

The lesson was that I needed to slow down. I needed to show my friends my appreciation. I needed to love on people. I needed to communicate better, just letting them know that I was challenged in my life right now, but that I valued their friendship. I also needed to apologize to own my humanness.

The second question was whether I learned the lesson, and the answer was a resounding yes. At first, I was defensive when I heard what she was upset about. I had all these reasons that I was rushed, but at the end of the day, that didn't change the experience for her. Once I got past being defensive about it in my own head and stopped justifying to myself all the reasons why I wasn't out of line, I realized yes, I absolutely was responsible here, that I had a role to play in this, that I had offended her. I'd learned the lesson.

Number three was: will feeling this way any longer benefit me? For days after I got the response from her, I felt physically ill. I beat myself up. We'd been friends for decades and I asked myself, "How is it fair that I was cut off from communication? Wouldn't a friend let me know that I'd screwed up, or let me know they didn't feel appreciated? Why didn't I get a chance to defend or explain myself?"

I realized that I'd felt sick about this situation for days even after I apologized. I was really feeling the lesson. I'd learned it and there was just no benefit to me continuing to wallow in this feeling.

Last, the bonus question. Does this relationship with this person allow me to feel my ideal BE state? For me, that means does it allow me to feel relaxed, abundant, and joyous?

I realized when I got past that emotion, on the other side where I'd taken responsibility and learned the lesson, I asked myself, "Does a friendship with someone who will cut me out of their life without communicating to me why serve where I'm going?"

I may have outgrown the relationship that was based on a shared history, and the relationship wasn't bringing out the best in me. I was taking radical responsibility for my experience and realizing this relationship was not allowing me to show up as the best version of myself. She deserved the qualities of having a friend who made her feel important and I deserved to be given grace when I was falling short. If we couldn't deliver those things to each other in this relationship, then neither of us was serving the relationship.

I am not suggesting that every time a relationship needs work, you let it go. In deep relationships, there are always going to be times where it's hard and requires effort to learn more about ourselves and each other.

However, a past relationship with someone does not guarantee a future. We can be very grateful for the role someone's played in our life, but also realize that it doesn't necessarily warrant that same energetic space going forward.

The last lesson I learned from the situation was that I really need to practice the Platinum Rule. You have all heard about the Golden Rule, which says that we should treat others as you would want to be treated. The Platinum Rule, though, is to treat others as *they* want to be treated.

MR. MISMATCHED

My senior year of college, I met a guy on Match.com. This was in the early 2000s, a *long* time before online dating was the norm. I was finishing my senior year in Oregon, and he was living in Southern California.

The first few months of long-distance phone calls and a few trips were exciting and romantic, and when I moved to California from Oregon, we started spending most of our non-work time together.

The warning signs began to flash: impatience, anger, ingratitude.

I had a moment of clarity a few months into dating and tried, unsuccessfully, to end it. Promises to change were made, my "fixer" mentality kicked in, and I was sure that if I could just love him enough, it would help him change.

And even though the warning signs escalated, I kept justifying that his love for me (even if expressed in a way that I didn't align with) was reason enough to stay, to keep trying. For five long years.

Had I understood my ideal BE state on that warm summer night in 2002, the breakup conversation would have been shorter. It would have been final.

Your BE state doesn't have room for anything but wishing others to be in their ideal BE state, just not at the expense of your own.

MR. RIGHT NOW BECOMES MR. RIGHT

In 2011, I met *the* guy, Igino. It wasn't the hammer to the head kind of thing (those emotions upon meeting usually result in an emotional hangover), it was the quiet thought of "this could be something" when he asked me on a second date while on our first date.

In the first few months, I'd had enough time together to realize we were extremely compatible, we had aligned values and goals, and we were both open to life and experience mixed with a zesty dose of curiosity and focus on personal growth. The fact that he was 6'8", looked like a Greek god, was incredibly educated, employed, *and* humble was the vegan icing on my gluten-free cake.

Years before, after a tumultuous break-up, I had written down all of the qualities I wanted in a partner. And Igino had them and then some. But I had never memorialized the way I wanted to *be* and *feel* with a partner. I didn't know it then, but he was triggering some serious BE states of connection, relaxed fun, joy and excitement without instability!

That little voice started saying, "He's the one."

Eight weeks into dating, on a quiet Sunday night, he told me he was moving back home for a job opportunity too good to pass up. He was 27 and less than a year single from a five-year relationship, with a move impending but not scheduled. And he didn't want to do long distance when he moved.

I was 31 and divorced, followed by an even more toxic relationship, and then spent 10 months with my last boyfriend going through Stage IV cancer. My ideal life timeline was derailing quickly.

I had the choice to break it off then before I became further emotionally invested or throw caution to the wind and proceed ahead. I'd had more fun and joy with him in eight weeks than in my previous decade of dating. It wasn't a hard decision. On top of all his other great qualities, he'd introduced me to good beer and hot sauce.

BUT REALLY, NO PRESSURE TO BEING MR. RIGHT – I'M JUST ENJOYING YOU BEING MR. RIGHT NOW.

I knew that focusing on what I couldn't control was a recipe for craziness. I didn't want to go down the obsession rabbit hole. So I focused all of my energy, time, and intention on *being* in the moment, of being fun and loving and connected to him. And we were!

I had my moments that the self-doubt or need to control and know the outcome crept in, when just hearing Adele's "Someone Like You" could send me into a crying fit. Or of wondering what I could *do* to change his mind about long distance.

But most of the time, I just focused on the BE. Without expectation, because there wasn't any, except to relish, savor, and enjoy every moment we had together. To not take it for granted, because I knew they were finite. To treasure them and wrap them up to enjoy after I watched the lights of his U-Haul fade into the sunset.

And in that BE state, I was so confident in our connection and compatibility that the idea of us not being together wasn't something I could even imagine. I worried *less* about it because I wasn't living in a state that a reality of us apart existed.

And our relationship grew. Our love grew. And six months later, the move date was scheduled. Six months of so much richness, intimacy, laughter, adventure, and experience. We boated together on the weekends, I played pit crew for his racing hobby and he attended my ballroom dance competition. He loved that I read books at night and I loved that he actually had better grammar than me.

As the date drew close, the inevitable couldn't be ignored. And in no reality could I imagine did he move off and become "the super healthy relationship I *had* with that incredible man who had to move." So a few weeks prior, I had an idea for what the future could look like that really could be the solution.

I proposed that we continue to date after he moved, but also date other people. *What?*

My intuition rational: if I were really that confident in our love and connection, we didn't need rules. I knew how I felt. I wasn't coming from a place of lacking. I wasn't living in a fear state. And I knew it would illuminate our future quickly. And while I wasn't thrilled about the idea of him going on a date with someone else, I was looking at the big picture of our future.

There were three possibilities.

1. If he was excited about dating other women and had fun, I wasn't the one. He'd know after a few dates, and then we'd move on with our lives.

2. If I was the one but the timing wasn't right, he'd be excited to go on dates, but something would be missing. And we'd work on the timing issue.

3. If he wasn't excited about dating other women, it would answer the question for him, without pressure or constraints on my part.

By being truly abundant, connected, communicative, and relaxed (well, as relaxed as you can be having this discussion with the one you love), he was open to long distance. Instead of looking at it for its challenges, I looked at the situation for the opportunity of adventure, travel, and being able to be incredibly connected on the weekends, then be in serious productive mode during the work week.

Many of the complaints people have about relationships (they get into a routine, they don't see their friends) were opportunities to have the best of both worlds here! And as I watched his U-Haul taillights fade into dusk, I knew it wasn't goodbye.

The next weekend, the first weekend of our Long Distance Vacationship, he told me he didn't want to date anyone else. It hadn't taken a date with someone else. It had just required me to be in my ideal relationship state of connection, support, understanding, positivity, and fun. And it allowed him to be clear in his (and my) role in that.

Now, disclaimer. This doesn't mean you should act "as if" with the guy you're seeing (or crushing on) by showing up with a suitcase and moving in. Or asking him about wedding venues.

Do we want to feel butterflies? Of course. Are relationships about give and take? Absolutely.

Understanding your BE state in a relationship is *vital*. It can help us not only get past that butterfly/sick to my stomach feeling (in 6 seconds or less), it can also rev up a relationship that might have gotten a bit stagnant when you weren't putting the intention and energy there.

In the beginning of a relationship, listening to your intuition can be *really* hard over the sound of all of those butterflies flitting around. So ask yourself the following and really listen to your intuition answering.

TOOLS FOR *BEING*, #26
RELATIONSHIPS

1. Is this someone I can be in my ideal BE state with?

2. Does a future with them align with your BE state?

3. When you're in your BE state while you're together, is that in line with their BE state?

CHILDREN

I now understand what people mean when they say their child is their greatest teacher. My first child taught me that in order to raise him to become the person I hope him to be, I must first be that person.

The only way for me to teach him generosity is to show him generosity to everyone.

To teach him to be patient, I must be patient.

To teach him to work hard, I must work hard.

To teach him to have an open mind, I must have an open mind.

To teach him to be healthy, I must be healthy.

To teach him to love, I must love.

To teach him to inspire, I must inspire him.

MY LITTLE MIRROR

When Luca was two, I walked into my bathroom to find him sitting and "shaving" his legs with my razor. First, I couldn't believe he'd reached it, or second, that he had any idea what to do with it!

It's a big reminder that children are constantly watching us and learning from what we do, not just what we say. They are modeling us, and often, the behaviors we love or don't love are a reflection of what is going on in their environment.

It's a reminder to constantly be working on *being* my best self. To ask myself how my best self would respond to a situation, especially when my default is a stressed response.

We all want to be the best parents for our children. In fact, our job and our privilege is to be for our children.

SOMETIMES, WE NEED HELP TO BE.

Transitioning from a family of three to a family of four has been *full* of transitions. Bedtimes, juggling the needs (and sometimes cries) of two at once, redoing our schedules again and again (and still going moment to moment with a teeny-ish one).

The biggest thing that I've learned from becoming a mom to my second is accepting *help*. Graciously. And even asking for it.

With my first, I still had an idea I could be super mom. That I could do it all. That I could juggle my own business, 100% care of my kiddo, a social life, passions, hobbies, and more all on my own. I'm not sure why I thought there was this badge to be won, but there wasn't.

At times, I did it. But more often, I felt like I was failing someone. Often, it was myself, as I ended up frazzled or exhausted. I finally understood the idea that you can do it all, just not at the same time. Or at least, not well. Something had to give.

This time around, I'm so happy when people offer help. Whether it's as simple as opening a door for me or holding my kiddo so I can use the bathroom or my in-laws offering to watch the kiddos while they nap so the big guy and I can get away for a short date.

And I discovered that accepting help didn't make me less than, weak, or less of a super mom. Quite the opposite. Receiving lets you give more. More to my kids, more to my husband, more to those around me. More to myself. More to others that need help too.

Don't be afraid to accept help. Don't be afraid to ask for it. It doesn't make you any less super, it makes you human. And that's a wonderful thing.

BEING IN THE MOMENT - ON DEMAND

Have you ever found a photo of yourself or someone you love that brings you back to that very moment? It's such a gift, a little moment of time travel back to feeling happy or excited or grateful.

We can give ourselves this prompt purposefully, and for me, looking at photos with my kids in their happiest moments, is one of the most effective tools to BE.

I do it when I'm in my flow state, loving what I'm doing, so I can be grateful I have abundance in every area of life.

I do it when I'm stuck, to give me inspiration and remind me that life is wonderful.

I do it when I'm frustrated, to center me back to what's important.

I do it when I don't want to work on something, to remind me who I'm the example for.

I do it when I do want to work on something non-stop, to remind me why breaks are important.

TOOLS FOR *BEING*, #27
VISUAL REMINDERS

Find a few favorite photos of your child or children, ideally captured in their BE state! Put them in places that you can use reminders to BE (on your visor mirror, bathroom mirror, desk drawer at work). When you are feeling a negative emotion like frustration, anger or lacking, look at that photo and visualize them in their BE state. How do you respond to it?

_____

_____

_____

LOVE LETTER TO MY LITTLE GUY...

You've got your own way that you follow without hesitation. Your courage, zest for life, and sweetness fill my heart.

You don't conform, which causes me encouragement, but sometimes, moments of frustration. That's my expectations needing to change, not *you* needing to change.

One of my greatest hopes for you is that you stay strong in who you are and never let the pressure to be the norm sway you from following your heart and soul calling.

As your mama, I vow to keep challenging myself to grow, so that I can not only tell you to be true to you, but so I can better show you with my own actions.

TOOLS FOR *BEING*, #28
A LOVE LETTER TO YOUR CHILDREN

Write a love letter to your children (or future children).

_____

_____

_____

_____

_____

_____

_____

_____

_____

_____

_____

_____

_____

_____

_____

_____

_____

_____

CHAPTER 12

Tools For Being You

"Love the life you have while you create the life of your dreams."
– HAL ELROD

The most talented carpenter in the world can have all of the knowledge to build something extraordinary, but without the tools, that knowledge will create little. And those tools are well used in building something that lasts.

In the same way, we must ensure we have the right tools to build the life we are designing. Below are some of my favorite tools in my toolbelt to designing and building a life I *love*!

MAGICAL MORNINGS - USING ROUTINE TO CREATE MAGIC

I was always a late-night person. In high school, it was staying up late agonizing over math problems (geometry never came easy for me). In college, it was bartending to pay my tuition and living expenses. And in my professional life, it was my time to catch up on e-mails or to finally unwind.

I admired those people who woke up at 5:00 a.m. but said "that isn't me." And so it wasn't. I identified myself as a night owl. And even when I heard an author and nutritionist say that the hours of sleep from 10:00 p.m. to 2:00 a.m. are the most vital *and* I recommended that to others, I wasn't living it.

Every attempt I made to join the 5:00 a.m. club was foiled, because I didn't *want* to get up. The title of being an early riser wasn't enough incentive to push off the warm covers and emerge into the cold, dark morning from my cozy bed.

Until I developed a magical morning ritual. Until I realized that the days that I didn't have me-time before my little guy woke up were days that I wasn't as relaxed, joyous, or abundant. That they were days that seemed rushed and busy, but not productive.

So it started by making my husband get me out of bed. (The exact instructions were, "It's not enough that I tell you I'm awake. I'll go back to sleep when you leave the room. You need to see feet on the floor.") Poor guy. But any grumpy grumblings were made up by my immense gratitude for that hour. And it only took a few enhanced days created by those magical mornings to no longer need his prompting.

That hour between 5:00 a.m. and 6:00 a.m. is when I do something decadent. Something unheard of in my reality of my first year as a mom. I spend an hour to myself. It consists of meditation with a candle burning, of doing my daily gratitudes, of stretching, of sipping my stress relief tea, and reading before the day has a chance to throw any stress my way.

That hour is *magical* for how it sets me up for my day. It's allowed me to be more purposeful, productive, and fulfilled. It's setting the destination in my navigation and filling the gas tank before the road trip that is my day.

Now, I can't *wait* to get up at 4:50 a.m. and get in bed before 10:00 p.m. for that delicious sleep before I intentionally begin my day.

With your current routine, do you feel prepared and excited for the day ahead, or rushed and behind from the moment your feet hit the floor?

What would you like your morning routine to be? What would support your ideal BE state as the foundation for your day? Pick three to five items from the list below or add your own.

Consider: meditation, gratitudes, affirmations, stretching or movement, self-care, time in nature, reading, listening to a podcast, free writing or journaling, enjoying a mug of warm tea.

Imagine the difference if you begin each day with this? How would you feel? How would you show up in your life? What would improve? What are the benefits, both short-term and long-term?

And what's the cost of not creating and committing to a morning routine that makes your day more purposeful, intentional, productive, and full of the qualities you want to live in? What won't happen or be experienced? How will you feel?

What changes do you need to make in order to honor your commitment? To see the benefits and to create a habit? Don't underestimate the power of a well-intentioned hour, or even 30 minutes, to change your day and your life!

TOOLS FOR *BEING,* #29
YOUR MAGICAL MORNING ROUTINE

What time do you typically get up? _____

What's your current morning routine? _____

_____

_____

_____

My Magical Morning Routine that supports my ideal BE state is: ___

_____

_____

_____

The benefit of designing, committing to and doing my Magical Morning Routine is:

_____

_____

_____

Changing nothing (if nothing changes, nothing changes) will mean:

_____

_____

_____

What changes do I need to make to my schedule or lifestyle in order to make my Magical Morning Routine sustainable? Going to bed earlier? Eliminating the glass of wine at dinner? Not looking at my phone or social media before my routine is complete?

_____

_____

_____

Lastly, who do you need to enlist support from to make it happen? Accountability is so important to lock in the change we want to see! Your significant other, roommate, children? _____

_____

_____

_____

☐ Check It off - Miracle Morning Completed!

MEDITATION

I spent most of my life in such *busy* action that the idea of slowing down to meditate seemed like such a waste. When I was introduced to yoga in my late 20s, I was introduced to the Savasana pose, or Final Relaxation

Pose, at the end of class. It's where you lay down, close your eyes, breathe naturally, and work to eliminate tension from your body. It's my favorite part of class and it's what made me open to meditation.

Now, when I feel to wound up or too busy to make time to meditate, I know I need that quiet more than ever. Meditation is probably the single most effective (and low-cost) daily tool I've found to train my brain, to lower my stress level and to get *really* clear on any answer I'm seeking. It also puts life wonderfully in perspective.

Our minds run fast, and in this day of the barrage of social media noise and connectedness that often leaves us feeling alone, we need more quiet and calm to just listen! To sort and sift all of the inputs, to just listen to our inner voice.

If you haven't meditated before, understand that it may be challenging initially. The goal isn't perfection, it's progress. Give yourself grace. My first six months meditating, it would take me eight minutes to get relaxed enough to feel the benefit of the last two minutes of the practice.

I love the apps Headspace and Calm for guided meditations. When I write, I go to YouTube and search Cosmic Vibrations to listen to sounds that provide a meditative experience while I'm allowing that inner voice to come through to paper.

 Meditation is wonderful first thing in the morning, and also right before sleep, when we can calm our racing thoughts and give the subconscious something to focus on throughout the night. But anytime you feel stressed, anxious or wound up, even five minutes can completely shift your state.

- Set a goal to meditate 5-10 minutes daily for one week!

  What did you notice? _____

  _____

  _____

  _____

GRATITUDE - HOW THREE MINUTES A DAY CAN CHANGE YOUR LIFE

If someone told you that you could do a three-minute exercise each day that would lower your anxiety, that would improve your sleep, make you happier, healthier and more confident, would you invest the three minutes?

The fastest, simplest and most proven method of changing your life is an integral part of getting into, and staying in, your ideal BE state. Gratitude!

While the word "grateful" gets thrown around a lot, it's not woo-woo self-help, but actual science. Expressing gratitude daily as an emotional and mental exercise is something I've been incorporating into my life for the past five years.

On the mornings that I do my gratitudes, the entire day just has a positive flow. And on the days that I forget or I don't prioritize it, the day has a tangibly different energy. When I notice that and stop what I'm doing to practice gratitude, whether it's 11:00 a.m. or 2:00 p.m., it's incredible how the day shifts after that.

Let's consider the reasons why we should practice gratitude. The first reason is psychological – because it leads to a happier you. Gratitude promotes positive emotions, helps you become more aware and more awake in your psyche, increases self-satisfaction and enhances mood. Why wouldn't we want all of those things?

Second are the physical benefits. Gratitude can build a stronger immune system, lessen body pains and aches, improve blood pressure and cardiac functioning, and create better sleep and wake cycles.

Third are the social benefits. Gratitude leads to better communication, more empathy with others, and stronger relationships. When you walk through life full of gratitude, people in group settings will find you more likable.

The fourth reason is because it aids in stress regulation. It reduces cortisol levels. High levels of cortisol actually suppress your human growth hormone, which is what controls our metabolism. In addition, gratitude reduces anxiety and depression and reduces aggression. You don't see a lot of Buddhist monks who are out getting in fist fights.

The Mindfulness Awareness Research Center of UCLA states that gratitude actually changes the neural structure of the brain to make us feel happier and more content. It alters the way that we see the world, and more importantly, the way that we see ourselves in the world (https://www.uclahealth.org/marc/default.cfm).

Now that we're fully convinced we *should* practice gratitude, the question is *how* we do it.

One is to take a few minutes when you wake up and again at bedtime to list three things you're thankful for from the day. Ideally, sync these times with something you do daily to create a habit. Practice gratitude in the shower, beginning with the hot water you're enjoying, the body that you're getting clean, the day you're starting. And continue on.

At night while you're brushing your teeth, for the warm bed you're about to get into, for the book you're about to read, or for the phone you're setting your alarm on. For the next day you'll wake up into.

Another method is to keep a gratitude journal. I personally have the five-minute journal, which prompts you to list your gratitudes as well as setting intentions for your day.

Gratitude is also one of the most effective tools to use in moments of frustration where you're overwhelmed and stressed. It's really easy to be grateful when things are going really well, but how many of us are grateful when things are going hard?

There is a saying that goes, "What you focus on grows. What you focus on, you attract." That's true, and when you move away from the focus of frustration and negativity and what's going wrong and focus on what's going right, more of it happens. Gratitude is a way to find the silver lining in the situation. When we shift our focus away from what is causing the stress and toward what we are grateful for, we realize that the problems are temporary and fixable. That mindset shift is so powerful. In addition, the gratitude feels so good. It doesn't take a lot of time, and the more you practice it, the better you get at making the shift.

The reality is that it's *easy* to be grateful when things are going great. Yet we still forget. However, how many of us are grateful when things are hard?

About three years ago, my husband and I took our son on his first international trip, and we were enjoying the exotic hustle and bustle of Barcelona on a two-week trip to Spain. On returning to our car, we saw that the back window had been smashed in. I had this sinking feeling as I realized our suitcase was gone out of the back seat, as well as our little travel bag with both of our laptops, iPads, my daily notebook and journal, my purse – everything.

Fortunately, I had my passport on me, but I knew that beating myself up or getting upset with my husband for parking in the wrong spot or because we didn't pack less to fit both suitcases in the trunk of the rental car, or that we should have kept our electronics with us, wasn't going to do any good. The theft had already happened.

I said a silent thanks that we were all okay and it was just a theft. It wasn't a mugging or a robbery and everything could be replaced. I focused on that gratitude while we were cleaning up the broken glass from the car seat. Gratitude that we were on this incredible trip. Gratitude we were safe. Gratitude we had insurance to cover the loss and money to cover the deductible.

Above all, in moments of stress, ask yourself, "What do I have to be grateful for?" The more you practice feelings of gratitude, the easier it will be to find those feelings even in moments when everything else seems hard.

If we get in the practice of expressing gratitude even when things aren't perfect, we focus on all that we do have. And any of us reading this post have internet, have power, and have a phone or computer, so we are in the top percentage in the world, wealth-wise.

Express gratitude for everything you have because you have the ability to. And then express more when more abundance comes into your life to be grateful for.

TOOLS FOR *BEING*, #30
GRATITUDE

Imagine that whatever you didn't express gratitude for each day was gone the next day. So you get up and you say, "I'm grateful for my family, my home, my health, my finances, even if they're not perfect. My job, my ability to choose, my pantry. I love my fridge. Electricity, shoes, sunshine." The list goes on and on. What if every day, you had to be grateful for each thing in your life in order for it to be there when you woke up the next day? How much time would you spend on gratitude then?

List Your Gratitudes! Imagine anything you don't list will be gone out of your life tomorrow. Forever!

Your Body

_____

_____

_____

_____

Your Home or Surroundings

_____

_____

_____

Your Relationships

_____

_____

_____

_____

Your Skills + Talents

_____

_____

_____

_____

Your Things

_____

_____

_____

_____

VISUALIZATION

Visualization is one of the most powerful mind exercises you can do. According to the popular book *The Secret*, "The law of attraction is forming your entire life experience and it is doing that through your thoughts. When you are visualizing, you are emitting a powerful frequency out into the universe."

Whether you believe it or not, we know that visualization works. Olympic athletes have been using it for decades to improve performance, and *Psychology Today* reported that the brain patterns activated when a weightlifter lifts heavy weights are also similarly activated when the lifter just imagined (visualized) lifting weights (https://www.psychologytoday.com/us/blog/the-psychology-dress/201111/visualize-it).

It's simple: *Your visualizations should focus on how you want to feel*, not just on things that you want.

What should you focus your visualizations on? Anything that inspires and motivates you. The purpose of your visualizations is to bring everything in them to life.

Again, remember the key about visualization that makes it so much more effective, and also moves you away from spending your valuable brain patterns on only achievement, is to visualize the feeling and the *being*, not the result of the being!

Instead of visualizing walking across a stage to accept an award, visualize the actions that you took to create the achievement. Visualize those actions happening in a relaxed, focused, and positive state.

Instead of visualizing the big paycheck, visualize the part of your business that creates the most value (and income) being easy and enjoyable.

Instead of visualizing the perfect body, visualize the feeling you get from nourishing your body properly and visualize the way you feel after a great workout.

 I find visualization to be easiest when I've mentally set the stage for it with meditation and affirmations first!

AFFIRMATIONS

Every thought is either an investment or a cost.
– T. Harv Eker

The idea of working out in order to have a fit, healthy body is an entirely accepted idea, yet the concept of working out our mind to have a positive, healthy mindset is so often overlooked!

Jack Canfield, author of **Chicken Soup for the Soul**, said "Daily affirmations are to the mind what exercise is to the body. Repeating affirmations helps to reprogram the unconscious mind for success."

While the idea of affirmations may be a bit cheesy to those who have never tried it, you'll soon become a believer, because affirmations *work!* They are a highly effective way to retrain or rewire your thoughts for more positive ones that create more possibilities in your life and eliminate negative and limiting beliefs!

If doing affirmations and feeling better isn't proof enough, there's even evidence from scientific studies using MRIs that positive affirmations work! Some of the benefits include decreasing stress, improving our health, and increasing academic achievement.

https://positivepsychology.com/daily-affirmations/

I've experimented with different ways to practice affirmations, so find what works best for you to incorporate into your day!

- Writing down one positive statement again and again, then reading it.

- Using an affirmation "deck" of cards and reading them out loud (and keeping out the ones I most want to work on throughout the day).

- Free speaking positive affirmations that come to my mind.

- Mixing speaking positive affirmations with movement of the body.

- Using an app that gives you positive affirmation prompts and then records you saying them to play back later.

TOOLS FOR *BEING*, #31
AFFIRMATIONS

How to create yours!

1. Use the words "I am" or "I believe" to begin your affirmation and speak in the present tense.

2. Make them specific and simple.

3. Keep them positive, focusing on what you want, not what you don't want.

I am _____ (your ideal BE state)!

I am grateful for _____ (love, health, relationships, etc.)

I am open to _____ (love, friendships, opportunities, money, etc.)

I believe _____ (in my potential, in my abilities, in my decisions)

Use the App ThinkUp to create and record your own affirmations set to music! I *love* listening to my affirmations (in my own voice) in the morning as I'm starting my day!

Adding affirmations into the mindset menu of meditation and visualization is going to supercharge your BE state and reprogram your brain!

TWO TIPS TO OWN YOUR TIME

Now you have the clarity for *being* and the tools for you! You've released obligations out of alignment with the life you're designing and you're ready to BE more instead of DO more.

Are you overwhelmed by a never-ending list of to-dos, or you spend the day working, but you find that you just don't accomplish every one of the important things you had on your list? You end up adding things to the list just to be able to check them off.

Or maybe you think multitasking is the answer to optimal time management. You're trying to load the dishes and listen to voicemails while responding to e-mails. I know, I had always considered myself a great multi-tasker. I'd have multiple projects and activities and commitments going on at once. While I usually finish the task, it was rarely my best quality, and worse yet, I felt constantly overwhelmed.

My husband, ever the engineer, told me for years that there's no such thing as multitasking. I didn't want to admit he was right, but I finally began to realize that my approach might not be the best, so I did a little bit of research on the effectiveness of multitasking. He was right! I learned it can actually decrease effectiveness, because your mind is pulled in too many directions at once. This is a hard pill to swallow, especially as a mom, if you pride yourself on multitasking.

This research led me to two techniques that revolutionized the way that I tackle tasks and what I am able to accomplish within a day. It has given me a renewed peace of mind as I work less, get more done, and actually enjoy my leisure time without being constantly obsessed or thinking about work while I'm not working.

The first tool is **time-blocking**. This means dedicating one block of time to one type of task. Time-blocking is a specific form of time management, but it really is designed to help alleviate the anxiety of this hectic day that we often find ourselves in. It also boosts productivity by directing our focus on the job at hand and off of all of the other things that pull our attention.

The first thing to do is get yourself a day planner and schedule everything that is important. That includes your appointments, your workouts or leisure time, your work, and anything else that requires your attention. If it's not on your calendar, it's not going to happen.

Instead of focusing on whatever's in front of you, you focus on batching similar tasks together. For example, you schedule one or two blocks of time to respond to e-mails each day rather than replying as requests come in. At the end of the day, someone else's e-mail is never as impor-tant as whatever you have planned. So don't let someone else's priorities overtake your agenda.

Plan a separate block of time to return phone calls. Phone calls require significant mental preparation, especially if you're in sales or you run your own business, so pencil in plenty of time. Even household tasks become quicker if you devote a specific time block to start and finish them, instead of leaving your home littered with all the half-finished chores.

Time blocking is excellent for "shallow work," the tasks we have that we could technically do even in a slightly distracted state, such as listening to music. This can be items like responding to e-mails, paying bills, and other housekeeping or administrative tasks. It's usually working "in" our business rather than on it and doesn't create much value for us.

An hour is typically the mind's maximum limit to stay focused, so make sure you block one hour or less and then give yourself a short break. That could be a great time to go have a snack or meditate or use the bathroom, because often if you like to book your calendar full, you're not scheduling in times for eating or your hygiene or brushing your teeth after lunch.

The second tool I want to share is the magic of **power sessions**. This is something I was introduced to a couple of years ago by my coach. This is where you carve out 45 to 90 minutes of a block of time without interruption. That means no phone calls, no e-mail, no social media or anything that's not related to the task you're dedicated to. A power session is where your goal is to create a dedicated block of totally uninterrupted time where you're going to complete one project, or step, from start to finish. It could be an entire project like launching a website or writing a blog, but it's sitting down and doing one thing from start to finish.

Power sessions are most effectively used for the "deep work." This is work where we can't be distracted, where we are often working on our business, not in it. It is work that creates significant value, such as writing or creating content, coming up with complex strategy, navigating and brainstorming through challenges. It is also what we often have the most resistance to and where we'll prioritize shallow work to feel like we got something done. But the deep work is what moves our lives and businesses forward.

Distraction is a one-way street that leads straight to unproductive busyness. Don't allow your mind to stray in several directions when you should focus on the assignment in front of you. Break that cycle. Set yourself up for success by scheduling that power session. The first day I did it, I wondered where it had been all of my life. It's really time management at its best. I also highly recommend putting your phone down, turning it over, or putting it in another room where you can't see it. It's so easy to pick that phone up and all of a sudden be in the scroll hole. So make a goal to complete three power sessions a day for a week.

Here are a few things to keep in mind. Your willpower and mental focus are at their peak at the beginning of the day. There is a concept called "eating the frog" which basically means doing the thing that is the hardest first. Leverage this time and tackle those big fires and your least favorite assignments in the morning.

Make the things that you want to do, that you're excited about, come at the end of the day. They are like dessert because you're going to want to do them anyway, but if you do them first, you're going to find that you put off the thing that's high priority. Again, schedule that high-priority task first, block the time to complete what's most urgent first, and it will reduce stress by taking the weight off the job that's on your mind.

Integrating these strategies into your life is going to be really easy. So now just sit down and schedule away.

TOOLS FOR *BEING*, #32
SHALLOW WORK

List all of the shallow work activities you do during the day. Consider e-mails/texts/Slack, returning phone calls, checking reports or statistics. _____

_____

_____

_____

Create 2-3 time blocks for shallow work during your day. Ideally, midday and end of day.

_____

TIP Don't start the day with a shallow work block, as it can throw off or distract you from your first deep work power sessions.

_____

List all of the deep work activities you do or would like to complete during the day! Creating content, developing strategy, sales calls. List your steps towards *big* goals here! _____

_____

_____

_____

Create three power sessions for deep work during your idea, including starting your day off with one and one right after lunch!

CLEAR THE NOISE – E-MAILS

You know how life gets distracting? How you have the best intention of checking so many things off your to do list, you get distracted, and suddenly it's 9:00 p.m. and you've done one thing (and that one thing you added to your list *after* doing it)?

There are only so many hours in the day, so we must be intentional with where we put our time and energy! What distracts you most for taking action?

For me, it's e-mail!! E-mails I'll file away to "read later" that take up mental space. E-mails I don't have time to read to even skim to see if I should file them to read later.

And there is an answer. And it is *free!*

About every six months, I go to www.unroll.me and I weed through my e-mail subscriptions. I prioritize what should come in my inbox, what should be rolled into a daily e-mail (non-urgent, non-important) and what I should say goodbye to forever (like four subscriptions to a yoga studio in a different state).

The result? A cleaner inbox, more ability to breathe and time to get things done that are actually important. Try it and share it!

CHECKING IN

It is so easy to get caught up in the *do* and to forget our intention for *being*, which is why it's *so* important to check in to help us stay in your ideal BE state!

I have a few questions I ask myself when I catch myself in that lower energetic state of frantic *doing!* I ask, "Am I being focused, feeling, and in flow in this moment?"

And usually, if I'm checking in, I am probably not being in that state. Then I ask myself:

Does what I'm currently doing support me *being* _____

How can I be more _____ in this moment?

When you're checking in often, it becomes so much easier to course correct. Suddenly, a few off-track minutes (or even hours) won't cause the entire day to be off track.

Soon after my daughter was born, when my nursing hormones were full-on, I had a situation where I got mom shamed. Someone who doesn't know me said something very negative about my parenting based on a photo on social media.

I was *very* triggered by the criticism, feeling anger, shame, and outrage. It would have been easy, and even understandable, to go down a rabbit hole of emotion, to reach out to others and retell the story to validate that I'm a great parent and that this guy was wrong!

What would that have accomplished? Kept me entirely out of the state required to be the best parent, to bring value to my work, to bring passion to what I do.

I checked in and I asked, am I being "relaxed, abundant, and joyous" in this moment? Hell no.

I asked, "Does doing more of looking at the Facebook comment to see other moms defending me, or telling other people what he said, support me in feeling relaxed, abundant, and joyous?" Again, a resounding NO.

Then I asked, "How can I be more relaxed, abundant, and joyous" in this moment? The answer was clear.

I decided to close my Facebook browser and re-center myself. I spent 10 minutes meditating and then doing affirmations that "I am a loving, joyous, wonderful parent."

Within 15 minutes, I was back into a state of feeling relaxed, abundant. and joyous.

TOOLS FOR *BEING*, #33
CHECK IN WITH YOUR EMOTIONS

The next time you are experiencing an emotion that doesn't support you, such as irritation, anger, boredom, sadness, *check in*. Ask yourself the below questions.

Am I *being* _____ (insert your ideal Be state here).

Does what I'm currently doing support me *being* _____ (insert your Ideal Be State here).

How can I be more _____ in this moment? (insert your ideal BE state here).

LETTER TO MY FUTURE SELF

In 2017, I attended a personal development workshop where we wrote a letter to our "future selves." I had just experienced a big breakthrough that I knew had the power to help me move past my perfectionist tendencies and the belief I needed to be busy and constantly achieving to prove my worth. The truth about breakthroughs is that it is easier to slide back into what is comfortable then create the change and putting the realization into practice that honoring the breakthrough will require.

When this letter showed up six months after the workshop yesterday, from the "past" me to "today" me, it was just the message I needed to hear. The reality is that after that breakthrough, when I was writing that letter, I was writing it *as* my future self. My best self, my highest self. The one that lives in an abundant, joyous, and relaxed state.

The Rebecca reading it had slipped back into some of her previous patterns. We are the ones with the answers we seek. We must stop and listen to ourselves instead of drowning out our inner voice with excuses, to-do lists, and noise.

My letter to myself:

"Your decision to focus has changed *everything*. You have channeled your creativity, positivity, ability, and potential into massive results.

You have impacted so many lives by focusing. You've finished your book, and with it, grown your impact. You're recognized as a lifestyle entrepreneur and brand expert.

Your focus on family has been the most impactful. Your relationship is the best it's *ever* been, and your husband and son feel special and valued. You are excited about your growing family."

The truth is that it took me *two years* more to finish my book. I'm still growing my impact. I'm still working on my relationship. My family has grown, and every day I express my gratitude for them.

Change may not happen overnight, which is why it's our responsibility and privilege to design that life and continue to work on becoming the person that loves living it.

TOOLS FOR *BEING*, #34
WRITE A LETTER TO YOUR FUTURE SELF

Write a letter to yourself 6 months from now

Go to www.futureme.org, and as your highest self, write yourself a letter.

I want you to describe your ideal BE state, the state you want to live in. Is it relaxed, joyous, and abundant? Is it connected, happy, and generous?

_____

_____

_____

How does your life look different? When you show up and you live in this state, how are you feeling? What is possible? What are you doing?

_____

_____

_____

How does it impact the people around you? And what does showing up this way and living this way allow you to experience? _____

_____

_____

_____

Who deserves this best you? How do you feel when you achieve the things that you want to do, but by being you in this state? What does becoming this person mean to you? _____

_____

_____

_____

 Choose when that e-mail shows up. Whether it's a month from now or a year from now, when you receive it, you may have forgotten that you wrote it. But I promise you it's going to show up when you absolutely need it the most.

BECOMING THE MOST WHEN YOU HAVE THE LEAST

I choose love. I choose joy. I choose to give. I choose to focus on growth. I choose to pour my time and energy into relationships that energize me.

In life, we will come across those who are threatened by our joy, our happiness, our love, and our success. Sometimes they will try to steal it.

But joy can't be stolen.

Taking it away from one person doesn't make the other more joyful. In fact, the absence of joy creates more absence of joy.

Our state of joy, of happiness, of love, of success, is something we have responsibility for. We can give joy to another and we receive it back multiplied. And in being joyous, we often share it, though there is no cost.

Many don't realize the most joyful people have often carried the heaviest burdens. We know the measure of a bad day. We choose to be joyful because we've felt the absence and we know that cost is far heavier. Stay strong and beautiful in your spirit, powerful in your stance, and keep changing the world – starting with your own.

Creating Impact Creates Legacy

Let me tell you a little something about a shake that changed my life.

It took me about 14 years of trying different things to find it (after VegaOne, raw diet, gluten-free diet, dairy free, no sugar, counting calories, counting macros, no alcohol, no red meat).

It took one phone call to hear the excitement in my friend's voice about her results (more energy, mental clarity, and fat loss), and to find out it was free of dairy, gluten, or anything artificial.

I made a decision to try it.

It took five days before I feel like someone had lit me up from the inside out.

It took 30 days to hit a goal I had estimated would take two to three months.

It took 60 days to start raving to my friends.

It took five days after they started to realize I wasn't that special, when I started receiving texts about how freaking good they felt. Goodbye, needing coffee to wake up. Goodbye, belly bloat.

It took me another 60 days to realize referring it to my friends (at the same price I was paying) had earned me more than six months of the products had cost.

It took 30 more days to attend my first event to learn a little more about the company, products, science, and social sharing opportunity.

It took me two hours of that event to feel like I'd found home. Something that excited me, that filled me with purpose, that gave me an exit from the path I was on that I didn't feel lit up about.

It took six months of *hard* work, of late nights, of working weekends with hundreds of conversations and phone calls to replace my corporate income and leave my job.

It's been five and a half years years since I retired from being an employee.

It's been six and a half years since I had that first shake.

I've helped about 450 people open up shopping accounts to purchase their own products at the same price I do.

So many people - more than 15,000 in nine countries - have said yes to their health as a result of those 400-ish people sharing.

I've earned over $800,000 in residual income.

I've taken about 25 trips that were write-offs that I chose to take to grow my business, several of them paid for.

I've made hundreds of friends that share a common purpose to help others feel and be their best.

I work that business 5-10 hours a week while raising two kids and running another company and diving deep into passion projects (like podcasting, writing and volunteering).

How many things will you consider trying?

How many looks will you take?

How many days are you willing to commit to living differently? It only takes one conversation to find out.

Go to www.rebeccacafiero.com/healthandwealth if you'd like to find out more or work with me.

Tools for Being

#1: The BE List

#2: Making Time to BE

#3: Aligning Your Goals with Your BE State

#4: Roadblocks

#5: Committing to your BE State

#6: Let's Let Go

#7: Your Non-Negotiables for Being You

#8: Plan a Day for Yourself

#9: What's Important to You?

#10: Check-in

#11: Phone Challenge

#12: Dream it + Be it

#13: Doing the Work

#14: The Power of Fire

Acknowledgements

This book would not have been possible without my husband, who saw me as an author long before I believed in that vision myself.

Kari and Cayla, for generously sharing your resources and even more valuable, your belief.

My editor Kelli, who lovingly pushed me forward to finishing my book, even at times when I struggled in *being*.

My nanny Kelly, who insisted daily I lock myself in my office to write and then brought me food and water!

My mentors and coaches who have helped me continue to quiet the noise so I could learn to share my voice and message.

My mom, from whom I became a book lover. And to my dad, from whom I became a storyteller.

My immensely talented and wonderful friend Molly, who always captures me *being* me.

For all of the people, friends and strangers, that have taught me how to BE..... Your impact on me is part of the fabric of who I've become.

I am grateful to all.